Puzzle Compilation: Jenny Lynch
Design: Theodore Szpindel
Editors: Amy Brem-Wilson and Simon Melhuish

Published by:
LAGOON BOOKS

ISBN 1-90281-378-2
© 2016 LAGOON BOOKS
Lagoon Books is a trademark of Lagoon Trading Company Limited. All rights reserved. Reprinted 2016.

Printed in China.

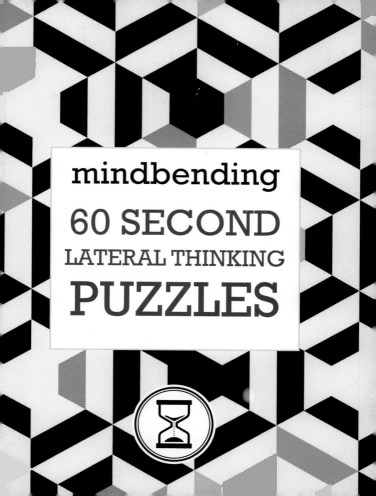

mindbending
60 SECOND
LATERAL THINKING
PUZZLES

ALL THE MINDBENDING PUZZLE BOOKS HAVE BEEN CAREFULLY COMPILED TO GIVE THE READER A REFRESHINGLY WIDE RANGE OF CHALLENGES, SOME REQUIRING ONLY A SMALL LEAP OF PERCEPTION, OTHERS DEEP AND DETAILED THOUGHT. ALL THE BOOKS SHARE AN EYE-CATCHING AND DISTINCTIVE VISUAL STYLE THAT PRESENTS EACH PROBLEM IN AN APPEALING AND INTRIGUING WAY. DO NOT, HOWEVER, BE DECEIVED; WHAT IS EASY ON THE EYE IS NOT NECESSARILY EASY ON THE MIND!

What do you put on the table, cut and then pass around, but would never actually eat?

Two miners were sitting on a bench. One miner was the other one's son, but the other one was not his father. Why?

A prisoner was made to carry a heavy sandbag from one side of the compound to the other. When he got to the other side, he had to take it back again. This went on, hour after hour, day after day, until the prisoner realised that he could put something in the bag that would make it lighter. What was it?

Which of the following
is the odd one out?

EGG,

FISH,

TABLE,

FOUNDATION,

BET.

I have two money boxes of exactly the same size and two types of coin. The small coins are solid gold and worth $10. The larger coins are exactly twice the size, contain twice the amount of gold and are worth $20. If I fill one money box with small coins and one with large, which will contain the greatest value when full?

My kind old aunt collects buttons, but even in an emergency she wouldn't let you sew any of them onto a garment. Why not?

I'm inside, halfway up a building that has no windows or balconies, yet I've got an incredible view of the city around me. What sort of building am I in?

Mr and Mrs Brown have got four daughters, who have each got a husband, two brothers and two sons. Can all the Browns fit into a 4 seater car?

Which one word can fill both gaps?

My _____ is _____ than my wallet.

The United manager was talking to his team after the match, when he pointed at Bryan Johnson, who was one of the laziest, most inept players on the pitch, and said, "If only we had five players like him." Has he gone mad?

How many times does the digit 3 appear between 1 and 50?

I had to meet an Australian, an American and a South African at the airport. One of them was called Bruce and I identified him immediately, despite never having met any of them before. How?

What can explode slowly, with no smoke or flame?

Look at the diagram below. What is it?

Why is Ireland different from Scotland, England, Wales and France?

Sheriff Tom Jones
rode into town on
Friday, stayed three
nights and left early
Sunday morning.
Explain.

I bumped into my long-lost uncle from Alaska in the street. I'd never met him, seen his picture or heard him described, yet I recognised him immediately. How?

How many times can you subtract 3 from 39?

Correct or incorrect?
The last woman to be hung in the UK was Ruth Ellis, who shot her love.

I went to France with something that stopped before we got to the airport. Despite this, it was still with me when I returned. What is it?

What object can you cut clean through and be left with one object with two ends?

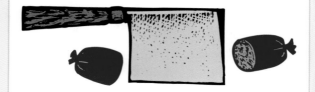

When the family jewels were stolen from inside a vat of vinegar and oil, my brother immediately suspected my sister's widow, but I knew this was wrong. How?

A man walks into a well-lit room and flicks the switch. The lights flicker and the man leaves, contented. Why?

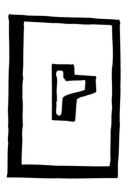

I've got ten or more daughters. I've got less than ten daughters. I've got at least one daughter. If only one of these statements is true, how many daughters have I got?

A father has three daughters who were all born on the 3rd of May, 1968. They are however not triplets. Explain.

What happened in Paris on June 31st 1945?

A prisoner survived
ten weeks in a cell
without water and with
a 20m thick steel door
between him and a
fresh water well in the
next cell. How?

When you're looking for something, you always seem to find it in the last place you thought of looking. There is a proven explanation for this. What is it?

What famous expression is this?

100S549A3
100F4E621T
0028Y2167

How many queens have been crowned in England since 1831?

What can move and be still at the same time?

A sphere's got three, a circle's got two, but a point hasn't got any. What?

"I cycled west from London to Bristol, stopping twice for a rest. I finished the journey in record time, helped along by gusting west wind." What is wrong with this?

A woman has three daughters who in turn, each have three daughters. If they all get together in one room, how many pairs of sisters are present?

My birthday is January 5th, but I always celebrate it in the summer. Who am I?

Which is true? One statement here is false? Two statements here are false? Three statements here are false?

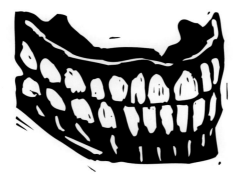

I bet you that if you stand on one end of my tie and I stand on the other, you will not be able to touch me. How?

I'm on earth, but I'm not in a time zone, nor am I between two time zones. Where am I?

At 8:34 precisely, on the day that President Nixon resigned, he looked out of a south facing White House window but couldn't see the top of the Empire State Building. Why not?

What is impossible to hold for half an hour, yet weighs virtually nothing?

At a family reunion one man went up to another. "Father!" "Grandad?" replied the other. Neither was mistaken. Explain.

In a balloon, stationary off the coast of Ireland, I dropped two wine bottles off the side. If one was full and the other empty, which hit the ground first?

They can be made, laid down, bent and broken, although it's difficult to touch them. What are they?

A professional footballer bet me that he could kick a ball a certain distance, have it stop, and then come back to him, without anything else touching it. He won the bet. How?

If you are walking forwards, but travelling backwards, and the only motion is being provided by you (not on a train, in a river etc.), where are you?

HOROBOD is a clue to the identity of a famous historical figure. Who is it?

A woman has three daughters who in turn, each have three daughters. If they all get together in one room, how many pairs of grandmothers and granddaughters are there?

What mathematical symbol can you put between 2 and 3 to make a number greater than 2, but less than 3?

Which English word do Australians always pronounce incorrectly?

How can I not sleep for 10 days and not be tired?

I was told by a magician to repeat "lemon" three times, so I said "Lemon, lemon lemon", whereupon he angrily said "Didn't you hear what I said?" What should I have said?

Antonio was a virtuoso musician who had never touched an instrument or written a note of music in his life. Explain.

A prisoner is kept on 50 grains of rice and a bowl of water a day. Despite getting progressively weaker, he manages to pull the bars from his window and escape after a year. How?

Look at the diagram below. What is it?

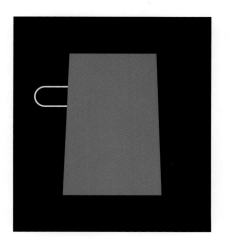

My grandmother is one of the sweetest, politest and most generous people I know, so imagine my surprise when I found a book in her house called "Go to Hell". On closer inspection, I realised my error. Explain.

If a clock takes 2 seconds to strike 2 o'clock, how long will it take to strike 3 o'clock?

How many string quartets are there in a dozen?

A victorious football team return home as champions of Europe. Their 1km long entourage moves at a rate of 1km/hour through the crowded streets. How long will it take to pass completely through the 1km long main square?

I have 25 hankies, equally divided into five different colours. If I were blindfolded, how many would I have to pick to guarantee having one of each colour?

In a pig sty, each of the sows can see an equal number of sows and male pigs, but each male pig sees twice as many sows as male pigs. How many pigs are there in total?

At midnight it is raining hard. How probable is it that it will be sunny in 72 hours time?

I'm in a tent, but it offers no protection from the wind, rain or snow, yet I don't want to leave it. Why?

What holds water, but is full of holes?

If aerosol propellants burn when lit, how is it that, when threatened by a snake whilst on a recent trip to the equator, I was unable to use my deodorant as a flamethrower?

If four boys can pick four apples in four minutes, how many boys would be able to pick 100 apples in 100 minutes?

I have two buckets the same size. If I fill one with small pebbles and one with large stones, which bucket will be heaviest?

Dave looked under a table and saw a hand, completely detached from an arm. He looked over at Alan and although his fingers and thumbs were in place and his hands were attached to his arms, he knew the hand beneath the table must be his. He stood up and punched him. Why?

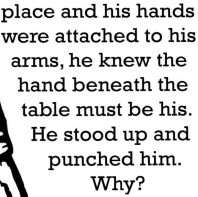

As I left the reptile house at the zoo I felt something move in my pocket. I put my hand in and discovered something with no legs and several teeth. Once I'd got over my initial surprise and had identified it correctly, I was happy to leave it there undisturbed. What was it?

What gets wetter as it dries?

Can you guess the next letter in this series?

C

Y

G

T

N

L

I

T

Racing driver Ramon Ricard had a terrible accident at Daytona leaving him in hospital for 6 months. Surprisingly, he never once considered giving up racing. Why not?

In a certain family, each girl has as many sisters as brothers but each boy has twice as many sisters as brothers. How many children are there?

I can stick a pin in a balloon without making a noise or releasing any air. How?

They are a dozen-strong gang, laden with jewels, weapons, internal organs and gardening equipment. Some of them are visually impaired, yet they have been sighted all over the place. Who or what are they?

Dave married two women, without divorcing either of them, or with neither woman divorcing him, committing bigamy or dying. Explain.

Even though I have only a 25, a 10 and three 5 cent coins, I can still make 30 cents with two coins, even though one of them is not the 25 cent coin. How?

My favourite team
have won seven
times this season,
but they haven't
scored a goal.
Explain.

What do you break by saying its name?

I am standing on a bare stone floor and I am holding a very fragile, very brittle porcelain cup. I am certain, however, that I can drop the cup more than a metre without it breaking. How?

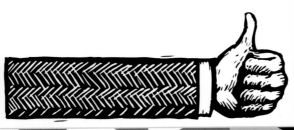

It was 3:30pm and sinister magician Umbro the Unnatural was standing in the middle of a park. There were no trees around him and not a cloud in the sky, yet he cast no shadow. How did he do this?

What's the smallest number of people you need to assemble two uncles and two nephews in the same place?

If I walked without an umbrella, or a raincoat, or a hat, across a treeless plain for an hour, how did I avoid getting wet?

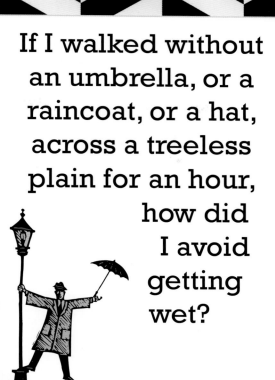

A man is killed by a pane of glass. The glass didn't fall on him and it wasn't broken before it killed him. So how did he die?

I can tie a knot in a piece of string without letting go of either of the ends. How?

solutions

Page 6
A deck of cards.

Page 7
She was his mother.

Page 8
A hole.

Page 9
You can't lay a fish.

Page 10
Despite the difference in size, you will get the same value of coins into each money box.

Page 11
She collects buttons from radios, televisions and lifts.

Page 12
A multi-storey car park.

Page 13
Yes. There are only four of them; Mr and Mrs Brown and their two sons. The other 16 have married names.

Page 14
LIGHTER

Page 15
No. United have played a disastrous game, and they would have fared better if only five of the players were as incompetent as Johnson, not all eleven of them.

Page 16
15 times: 3, 13, 23, 30, 31, 32, 33 (two 3s), 34, 35, 36, 37, 38, 39, 43.

Page 17
The other two were called Lucy and Mary.

Page 18
A population.

Page 19
A bird's-eye view of a man on a bicycle wearing a sombrero.

Page 20
It's got three vowels.

Page 21
Friday is the name of his horse.

Page 22
He is my dad's identical twin.

Page 23
Once. After that you're subtracting 3 from 36, and so on.

solutions

Page 24
Incorrect. People are hanged, not hung.

Page 25
A watch.

Page 26
Any sort of loop.

Page 27
My sister can't have a widow.

Page 28
He is an executioner, and came in to test the electric chair, which always makes the lights flicker.

Page 29
None. If "I've got at least one daughter" is true, then "I've got ten or more daughters" can also be true, and vice versa. "I've got less than ten daughters" can be true by itself, but only if I have no daughters.

Page 30
They are three of four quads.

Page 31
Absolutely nothing. June has only got 30 days.

Page 32
The door wasn't locked.

Page 33
It's always the last place because, once you've found it, you stop looking.

Page 34
SAFETY in numbers.

Page 35
None. Both Victoria and Elizabeth II were princesses when they were crowned.

Page 36
A carton of orange juice.

Page 37
Dimensions. A point is a place. It has no form.

Page 38
A west wind would slow you down if you were cycling to the west, as it blows from the west.

Page 39
12.

Page 40
Someone who lives in the southern hemisphere.

solutions

Page 41
Two statements here are false.

Page 42
If I thread my tie under a door, we wouldn't be able to touch each other.

Page 43
At one of the poles.

Page 44
Because the White House is in Washington and the Empire State in New York.

Page 45
Your breath.

Page 46
The grandson was a priest.

Page 47
Neither hit the ground. I was over the sea.

Page 48
Rules.

Page 49
He kicked it straight up in the air.

Page 50
On a log, a large ball, or any spherical or cylindrical object.

Page 51
Robin Hood. ROB in HOOD HO(ROB)OD.

Page 52
There are 9.

Page 53
A decimal point.

Page 54
Incorrectly.

Page 55
By sleeping at night.

Page 56
"Lemon, lemon, lemon, lemon." If he'd told me to repeat "lemon" once, I should have said it twice.

Page 57
He was a singer.

Page 58
Every day he would save and dry a couple of grains of rice, put them in the cracks around the bars and pour some water on them. Gradually the swelling increased the size of the cracks and loosened the bars.

Page 59
A Trombonist in a portable toilet!

Page 60
It was the sixth volume of an encyclopedia.

Page 61
4 seconds. If the time between the clapper striking the bell for the first peal and the second peal is 2 seconds, then it will be a further two seconds before it strikes for the third peal.

Page 62
12.

Page 63
Two hours. The front of the procession will take an hour, and will be leaving the square just as the tail-end enters it.

Page 64
21.

Page 65
Four sows and three male pigs.

Page 66
72 hours later it will be midnight.

Page 67
I'm in an oxygen tent.

Page 68
A sponge.

Page 69
I use roll-on deodorant.

Page 70
Four. As a team, they can, on average, pick one a minute.

Page 71
They will both weigh the same – surprisingly, no matter what the size of the stones the proportion of stone to air space remains the same.

Page 72
They were playing cards. The "extra hand" was a set of duplicate cards, proving that Alan was cheating.

Page 73
A comb I hadn't seen in a while.

Page 74
A towel.

Page 75
S. They are the first letters

solutions

of each of the words of
the question.

Page 76
Because he fell down
some stairs.

Page 77
Three boys and four girls.

Page 78
The balloon isn't inflated.

Page 79
A pack of cards.

Page 80
Dave is a priest who
conducted two weddings.

Page 81
By using a 25 and a 5 cent
coin. Although one of them
is not the 25 cents, the other
one is.

Page 82
It is a cricket team.

Page 83
Silence.

Page 84
If I hold the cup 2 metres off
the ground, it will fall 1.99m

without breaking. The final
0.01m will, however, cause it
to shatter into tiny pieces.

Page 85
It was a winter's afternoon
in Scotland and it was
already dark.

Page 86
Two. If two men marry
each other's mothers, they
automatically become
half-brothers. So, if they
have one son each, then
the other one's son is
automatically nephew
and uncle!

Page 87
It wasn't raining.

Page 88
He fell through it from a
great height, rather than it
falling on him.

Page 89
By picking up the string with
my arms folded, and then
unfolding them.

We are indebted to a number of fellow puzzlers and thinkers who have provided us with inspiration for this book, in particular, Paul Sloane and also Dr. Edward de Bono, Boris A. Kordemsky, Victor Serebriakoff, Martin Gardner, Trevor Truran, Des MacHale & Dr. Diana Taylor.

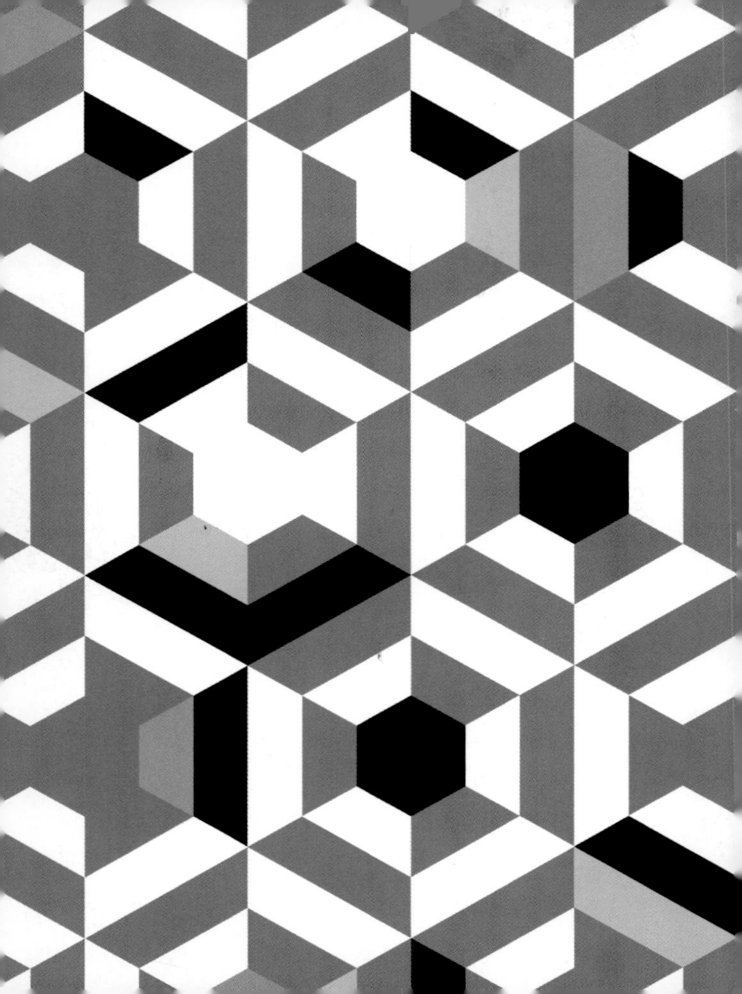

MANCHESTER CITY

A RANDOM HISTORY

An exclusive edition for

This edition first published in Great Britain in 2023 by Allsorted Ltd, Watford, Herts, UK WD19 4BG

© Susanna Geoghegan Gift Publishing
Author: Magnus Allan
Cover design: Milestone Creative
Contents design: Bag of Badgers Ltd
Illustrations: Ludovic Sallé

ISBN: 978-1-915902-06-1

Printed in China

★ CONTENTS ★

"IF YOU'RE GOING TO WIN THE PREMIER LEAGUE, YOU'RE GOING TO HAVE TO FINISH AHEAD OF CHELSEA AND MANCHESTER CITY."

Graeme Souness makes an exceptionally good point (while also neatly showing how the balance of power has changed over the last couple of decades).

★ INTRODUCTION: ★

THE GAME OF TWO HALVES

Let's get this over and done with before we go any further: there are two Manchester Cities. The first existed before 2008, a team that had tasted glory in the 1960s and 1970s, but was mostly holding on to the Premier League by the tips of its fingers, making regular visits to the Second Division (whatever that decided to call itself in any given season).

Then there is the recent Manchester City. A club that attracts world-class talent and uses alchemy to make that talent part of a team that plays sublime football. A team that terrifies virtually every other team in Europe. A team that everyone wishes they supported.

The thing is, though, it's a bit easy to roll your eyes and shrug at City. Yes, they've had a massive change in the amount of funds available, but they've also worked hard, made a lot of the right decisions and had their fair share of luck over the last few seasons.

There is a long list of teams that manage to attract exotic megabucks investment, bring in exceptional talent and build shiny new stadiums, only to quickly trip themselves up or for the investment to turn sour. Take Valencia, a team that, for a brief moment, was going to challenge for dominance in La Liga with a swanky new world-class stadium that has stood, half-built and silent, for nearly a decade and a half. Or closer to home, look at one of the teams in west London that has spent and spent and spent over the last season or so but still can't find a way to turn their talent into a team. Won't mention names, but they play in blue and they've been doing the same thing every once in a while since 1905.

Even closer to home, look at how quickly the bright days of 2007 dimmed into a potential crisis in 2008 for City ...

Over the decades, City fans have endured bad times and worse. They've been frequently forced to deny that there has been any envy about what's happening down the road in Salford, out west along the M62 or in various parts of London. In some ways, after four decades of turmoil, it started to feel like it was probably City's turn to have some time in the limelight. The thing is, though, football – like life itself – doesn't work that way.

Right now, for whatever reason, it has gone right for City – and, for as long as it continues, it is time to bask in the glory of being a Manchester City fan.

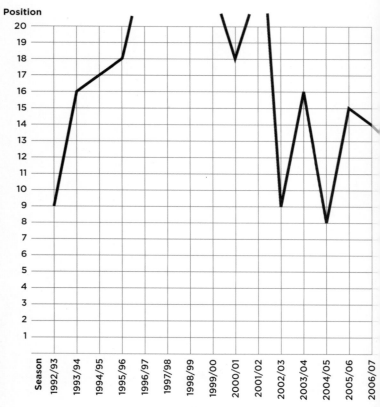

·MANCHESTER CITY·

Position

Season

1992/93 1993/94 1994/95 1995/96 1996/97 1997/98 1998/99 1999/00 2000/01 2001/02 2002/03 2003/04 2004/05 2005/06 2006/07

8

PREMIER LEAGUE
★ FINAL POSITIONS ★

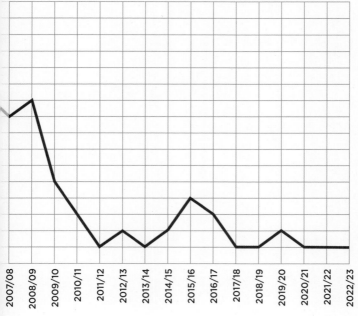

★ TOMMY JOHNSON ★

10

Tommy Johnson scored in the first match at the Maine Road stadium in 1923 – one of the 158 league goals he delivered in his 328 league appearances during his 11-year Manchester City career.

He'd joined City in 1919 as the Football League got back on its feet after World War I, but only made sporadic first team appearances during his first few years, particularly because Horace Barnes and Frank Roberts tended to be picked ahead of him.

By the 1925/26 season, though, he was fast becoming the main draw, but in a tale that will be all too familiar to longer-term City fans, his 20 goals weren't enough to keep the team in the top flight.

The next season, he provided 25 goals as the team fought tooth and nail to get back into the First Division. Despite it going to the wire, and winning 8–0 on the final day of the season, they were pipped to the post and had to endure the ignominy of a second season in the Second Division. The disappointment would not be repeated, however, with City rising back to the First Division as 1927/28 Second Division champions.

The next season, Johnson found the net 38 times in 39

league appearances, a record that stood for nearly a century, until it was beaten in 2023 by Erling Haaland. Johnson scored five of City's six goals against Everton in 1928 (which is also something that Haaland is welcome to try and crack at some point if he fancies it. Not just against Everton, anyone he likes really).

Johnson, meanwhile, made five appearances for England between 1926 and 1933, scoring five times. He scored 166 goals in all competitions for Manchester City and is still the team's third-highest all-time goal scorer.

He left City for Everton and then saw out his playing career as player-manager at non-league Darwen, before returning to Manchester to run pubs in Stockport and Gorton.

"MY SUPER STRENGTH IS SCORING GOALS. A LOT OF IT IS BEING QUICK IN THE MIND AND TRYING TO PUT IT WHERE THE GOALKEEPER IS NOT. I WAS SO TIRED AFTER MY CELEBRATIONS."

Erling Haaland reminds us that he's still very young and sometimes needs a little nap after all those goals.

13

STRAIGHT OUTTA
★ GORTON ★

Back in the mid-19th century, society had a problem. In cities and towns up and down the land, the youth had turned to violent crime. Boredom, booze and the breakdown of traditional family relationships were to blame, and the upshot was that in cities like Manchester there were gangs of youths running wild, causing mayhem and committing crime. Which are three sides of the same coin really.

It was a common theme in social commentary at the time, with Manchester's neighbourhood-based scuttling gangs attracting particular attention. At one point, it is said that Strangeways Prison had more inmates that had been arrested for youth violence and scuttling than for any other reason. There were the usual headlines in the papers, and politicians offering their considered insights, but a few people decided that sport might offer some of the gang members a distraction and a way to improve themselves.

It's easy to think of the mercantile class of the mid- to late-19th century as seeing the deprivation in industrial towns and cities, tutting, wringing their hands and not doing a lot, but several of them donated extensively to churches as a way of helping their communities (and, if you were cynical, polishing their halos – although, in the final analysis, why not both?). In turn, many of these churches became centres of the local community and helped try to give the lives of at least a few of the urchins in cities like Manchester a bit of a structure. It wasn't something that the governments of the day involved themselves with, but scuttling gangs and their ilk across the country show it really was something that needed doing.

St Mark's, in the west of Manchester's Gorton area, was one such church. It founded a cricket team in the late 1860s and then, a decade or so later, many of the members of the cricket team formed an association football team. Tottenham Hotspur, coincidentally, went through a similar development process (although without the church involvement).

It may be that the level of gang-related disruption in Manchester at the time meant that local newspapers were quick to cover any positive impact of the various sports teams that were emerging in Manchester and across the north of England. Or it could simply be that football sold newspapers from pretty much day one. Either way, the exploits of the St Mark's (West Gorton) association football team got plenty of coverage as they made their way through the early days of the sport.

THE FIRST MONDAY NIGHT FOOTBALL GAME SHOWN ON SKY DURING THE FIRST SEASON OF THE PREMIER LEAGUE IN 1992/93 WAS MANCHESTER CITY AGAINST QUEENS PARK RANGERS. (1-1, HAPPY DAYS.) SKY ALSO EXPERIMENTED WITH BRINGING IN CHEERLEADERS, THE SKY STRIKERS, TO LIVEN UP THE MONDAY NIGHT CROWD. WAS IT A SUCCESS? DO SKY STILL HAVE CHEERLEADERS?

"IF I WASN'T PRAYING FOR CITY, JUST THINK WHERE WE MIGHT BE."

Chaplain Tony Porter
brings religion and logic
to City in the 1990s.

★ ERIC BROOK ★

Eric Brook was by trade an outside left, but, by all accounts, he was at his happiest when he was given the freedom to roam the football field, popping up to receive balls wherever it made the opposition most uncomfortable. The left wing was simply somewhere he stood at kick-off.

He came to Manchester City from Barnsley in a joint signing with Fred Tilson in 1928, and the pair enjoyed a devastating partnership for several years, jointly responsible for 310 goals in 726 matches.

Brook had an eventful 11 years with City, helping them win promotion back into the First Division in 1927/28, lifting the FA Cup in 1933/34 and then crowning it all as league champions in 1936/37.

Of course, this was City, so despite the team knocking in 80 goals the next season, more than any other team in the First Division, the team was relegated to the Second Division. It's not a great claim to fame, but this is the only time that the reigning top-flight champions have been relegated in the season after winning the league title. It's also the only time that a team has been relegated from the top flight with a positive goal difference. Which, again, is not great, but if you are going to collapse in a heap, you might as well do it with a bit of panache.

Brook became City's top scorer of all time in 1939, overtaking Tommy Johnson's 166 goals (see page 11), and his 177 goals held the record at the club for 78 years until Sergio Agüero took the crown in 2017 (see page 145). Agüero's gift for the achievement was presented to him by City legend Mike Summerbee (see page 61) and Brook's daughter, Betty Cowgill.

Brook played for England 18 times, a number that would have been higher were it not for strong competition for his position from Arsenal's Cliff Bastin and several others. There was also the small matter of England not involving themselves with the international footballing authorities for much of his career (a dispute about principles and money you'll be astonished to hear), which reduced the number of matches in which the national team played.

His career was ended by a car accident in 1940 as he was on his way to play for a wartime international against Scotland. The accident left him with a fractured skull, which meant heading the ball was seen as risky. If the medical profession was saying something was risky in the 1940s, they probably really meant it.

"HE RENTED MY HOUSE FOR A COUPLE OF YEARS AND HE ALWAYS MADE SURE IF ANY WORK NEEDED DOING HE WOULD DO IT."

Micah Richards suggests that David Silva was always handy with a paintbrush.

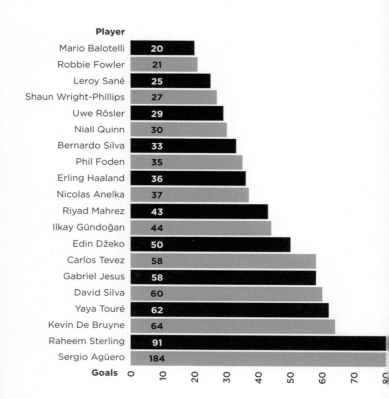

Player

Player	Goals
Mario Balotelli	20
Robbie Fowler	21
Leroy Sané	25
Shaun Wright-Phillips	27
Uwe Rösler	29
Niall Quinn	30
Bernardo Silva	33
Phil Foden	35
Erling Haaland	36
Nicolas Anelka	37
Riyad Mahrez	43
Ilkay Gündoğan	44
Edin Džeko	50
Carlos Tevez	58
Gabriel Jesus	58
David Silva	60
Yaya Touré	62
Kevin De Bruyne	64
Raheem Sterling	91
Sergio Agüero	184

Goals: 0, 10, 20, 30, 40, 50, 60, 70, 80

MAN CITY'S LEADING PREMIER LEAGUE ★ GOAL SCORERS ★

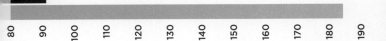

80 90 100 110 120 130 140 150 160 170 180 190

GORTON, ARDWICK, ★ THEN ... ★

The history of the club that became Manchester City is complicated. Despite the newspaper coverage of the games themselves, there is no clear paper trail available to track the various teams around Gorton that merged and split and merged again, although this may have been so that serious historians of the future could amuse themselves. However, the long and the short of it is that by 1887 Gorton Association Football Club moved to Hyde Road and renamed itself Ardwick Association Football Club. Details are scant, but it seems likely that part of the reason for the name change was because Hyde Road is in the district of Ardwick rather than Gorton.

The team developed an association with the Hyde Road Hotel, which was next door to their new playing field. The hotel's landlord, who was also a brewer, played an increasingly important role in the organisation of the club, supporting the building of the stadium and running its bars. Ardwick AFC's nickname was 'the Brewerymen' for a while.

The team enjoyed success, winning the prestigious Manchester Cup in both 1891 (defeating Manchester United antecedent Newton Heath in the final) and 1892, and then joining the newly formed Second Division of the Football League the same year.

Storm clouds were also brewing, though. Building a stadium isn't cheap, even when you have the support of a local brewery, and the game was slowly becoming more professional, with players increasingly expecting to be paid for their services.

Players also needed to be paid for their travel. In the closing years of the 19th century, getting round England could be slow and expensive. In the case of the Second Division, the 1893/94 season would have included away trips to Newcastle United in the north and Woolwich Arsenal in the south. In the case of the latter, this wasn't just a question of mooching south out of the Etihad, flicking on the cruise control and rocking up at the Emirates a few hours later. You not only had to get to London, but you then had to get across London to

Woolwich, which in the 19th century pretty much doubled your journey time (as opposed to quadrupling it, which is what it would do today).

So, anyway, paying for good players, giving them a home where they could perform and getting them to their away matches required sound finances, as Ardwick discovered to their cost. The team started to run up debts and, unfortunately, collapsed at the end of the 1893/94 season.

Fear not, though, good reader, because they were quickly reorganised, put on more solid financial footing and emerged, like a butterfly from a chrysalis, as Manchester City Football Club, never again to suffer the ignominy of being skint. Kinda.

"WE DREAM OF PLAYING IN THE SHIRT. TODAY GOD CHOSE YOU. PLAY LIKE THE DREAM,"

read a banner on display at the City of Manchester Stadium during a mid-season slump in 2004. You can never question the commitment of true City supporters.

★ ALEC HERD ★

Alec Herd joined City in 1933, just in time for the team to come second in that year's FA Cup final. The City team of the era made up for it, though, winning the trophy the next year and then becoming league champions for the first time in 1936/37.

On paper, the success wasn't perhaps all that surprising, given that the City team already boasted an array of talent including England internationals Jackie Bray, Eric Brook, Sam Cowan, Frank Swift and Fred Tilson, as well as former Scotland captain Jimmy McMullan. As football has shown time and time again, though, there's more to building a successful team than just throwing money about and bringing in a set of talented individuals – but succeed they did.

Herd made 257 league appearances for City, scoring 107 times despite World War II taking its toll on the length of his top-class playing career. After the war he joined Stockport United where he made 111 league appearances and scored 35 goals.

A M^CCRUM OF
★ COMFORT ★

The ancient Greek philosopher Anon once said penalties are the worst way of deciding a football match, except for all of the alternatives that have been tried from time to time (Churchill paraphrased the saying when talking about democracy – look it up). But while we all wince when a dubious penalty is not given, or given (anyone over the 1996 FA Cup quarter final against United? Thought not), and fret whenever extra time inexorably gives way to spot kicks, it's worth remembering that we've come a long way since the idea was first suggested.

Football's origins trace back to various forms of brutal anything-goes inter-village competitions that were sometimes allowed in feudal Britain. As the country industrialised and urbanised, there was less space in the cities and towns, so packs of players could no longer roam across hill and dale chasing a ball. Defined football pitches started springing up around the place.

In 1863, a group of schools and sports teams got together in south London and created a set of rules, basically because everyone played the game differently and they were getting sick of spending hours discussing the rules beforehand, rather than playing the game itself.

At this point, it was still perfectly legal to shoulder-barge a goalie into the goal if they were holding the ball (brutal perhaps, but it cut down on time-wasting).

By 1874, the men in black started appearing on the football field, and teams began to be awarded with indirect free kicks, although only if a defending team's outfield players handled the ball. At the time the box didn't exist – there was a simple 10.97-metres (12 yards; moan all you like, we went metric over half a century ago) line that ran side to side across the pitch and the goalie could handle the ball anywhere within that area.

Now, the English like to lord it up and claim that football was invented and popularised in this green and sometimes pleasant land, but it was an Irish goalkeeper who proposed that penalties should be added to the rules at the end of the 1880s. The gentleman in question went by the name of William McCrum, and he suggested that the beautiful game was being let down by too many professional fouls – that if an attacker was clear through on goal, some defenders tended to play the man, not the ball, to deny clear goal-scoring opportunities. And in a world without repercussions, you would, wouldn't you?

The proposal was widely dismissed as the 'death penalty' or the 'Irishman's notion'. Football was a sport played by gentlemen and didn't need to be governed in such minute detail said the detractors. Some even made the clearly ludicrous suggestion that attackers might start falling over at the lightest touch of a defender just to trick the referee into giving a penalty kick ... Just imagine.

The thing is, though, people kept getting injured and, with the greatest of respect to Victorian medical practitioners, even a broken leg could often be a terminal diagnosis. More importantly than the potential death of a player, clubs were maxing out their budgets to bring in the best players only to have them kicked out of the game on debut. This was irritating for coaches and accountants alike.

And so, at the end of the 1890/91 season, football started to see reason, and penalties for professional fouls became the official 13th law of the game. It's subsequently become the 14th law, presumably because penalties are difficult enough without the Football Association jinxing them.

The first penalties could be taken anywhere on the 10.97-metre (12-yard) line and the goalie was free to prowl anywhere they liked within six yards of the goal line. By 1905, the rules were tweaked again to create the penalty spot (technically called the penalty mark) and the box. At this point the goalie was confined to the goal line, formalising the whole process into pretty much what we know today.

Manchester City have taken 144 penalties during the Premier League era, finding the net around 80% of the time. The stats dropped in 2019/20 and 2020/21 to a little over 50% of penalties scored, but for the 2022/23 season have climbed back to around 90%. Which is a quietly glittering statistic and shows that Pep and his team look at all aspects of the game and change things when they need to.

★ BERT TRAUTMANN ★

You can put a lot into a game of football. It's all stories of beating insurmountable odds, of being part of something bigger, of redemption and forgiveness. Most of the time it's nonsense, it's just 22 people chasing a ball and each other around a field of grass. Sometimes though it really is about something else.

Bert Trautmann volunteered for the German army and fought as part of the war machine that tried to sweep across Europe in the 1940s. Captured by the British as the war came to a close, he discovered he had a talent for goalkeeping while being held at a prisoner of war camp in Lancashire. He stayed in the region after he was released, playing part-time for St Helens Town.

His reputation grew and he signed for Manchester City in 1949. He was initially very unpopular in a city that had been scarred by the war. More than 20,000 people protested his arrival, and it took the intervention of a local rabbi to calm the tensions. The rabbi's family had suffered significantly during the war, but he was still willing to call for forgiveness – and the people of Manchester started to come around.

After those difficult first few weeks, it was Trautmann's

ability as a goalkeeper that began to make headlines. He played an important role in the Revie plan, a strategy that broke from the norm of English football and led to City getting to consecutive FA Cup finals in 1954/55 (which they lost to Newcastle United) and 1955/56 which they won.

In that second final, as the minutes ticked by, Trautmann was knocked out in a collision with the opposition's inside left This was in the days before substitutes were allowed (and well before concussion checks were even discussed), so he had to either play on or consign City to playing with 10 men for the rest of the match. He struggled on, despite the fact that he could barely stand, playing "in a kind of fog" as he described it later. He made a couple more excellent saves and, 15 minutes or so later, City won the FA Cup for the first time since 1933/34. It was only the third time in the club's history that they'd won the trophy.

A couple of days later and his neck was still sore, so he made his way to hospital. They gave him an X-ray and then informed him that the collision with the opposition player had broken his neck. Lucky that he hadn't tried to shrug it off, really.

"HE'S PROBABLY ALREADY FORGOTTEN ABOUT THAT BANG ON THE NECK."

Commentator Kenneth Wolstenholme was basically one step away from telling Trautmann to run off his broken neck after the 1956 Cup Final.

THE GREATEST
★ MISSED PENALTY ★

There are several techniques for scoring a penalty and several ruses that goalies can employ to try to put players off, but one of the greatest penalty muck-ups came a century after the spot kick was introduced. During a match between Arsenal and Manchester City in 2005, Arsenal's Robert Pires stepped up to take a penalty against Manchester City after Dennis Bergkamp had been rigorously stopped in his tracks by City defender Stephen Jordan.

In a move that clearly hadn't been practised enough, Pires made his run up, but then tried to trick goalie David James by making a light tap to Thierry Henry who was steaming in from his left. It would have been perfectly legal if the ball had travelled forwards and as long as Pires only made one touch. Johan Cruyff had achieved it in 1982, playing a one-two with Ajax team-mate Jesper Olsen before tapping the ball into the back of the net. The way that Cruyff and Olsen make it work is both supremely cheeky and probably psychologically devastating.

Fortunately for City, Pires' tap was way too light, and Henry thundered past the ball like Wile E. Coyote missing Road Runner. When Pires tried to correct his mistake, he kicked the ball a second time, which is against the rules, and the referee awarded City a free kick while City's travelling faithful roared with laughter.

If you are ever having a bad day, it's well worth watching again. Actually, it's worth watching again if you are having any sort of a day.

CITY LEGEND MIKE SUMMERBEE HAD A SPEAKING PART IN 'ESCAPE TO VICTORY', THE DEFINITIVE WORLD WAR II FILM ABOUT FOOTBALL.

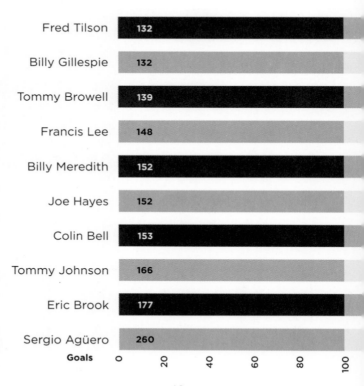

·MANCHESTER CITY·

Player	Goals
Fred Tilson	132
Billy Gillespie	132
Tommy Browell	139
Francis Lee	148
Billy Meredith	152
Joe Hayes	152
Colin Bell	153
Tommy Johnson	166
Eric Brook	177
Sergio Agüero	260

Goals   0   20   40   60   80   100

MAN CITY'S LEADING ALL-TIME GOAL SCORERS

★ ★

(ALL COMPETITIONS)

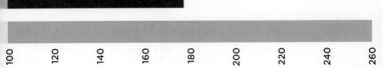

100   120   140   160   180   200   220   240   260

• MANCHESTER CITY •

LES McDOWALL

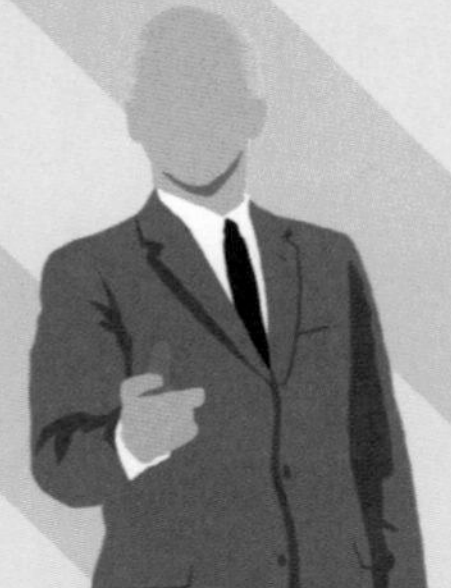

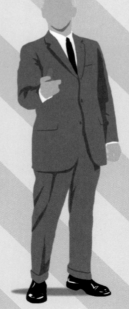

If you overlook the small matter of three appearances as player-manager for Wrexham, Les McDowall moved neatly from a war-interrupted 12-year playing career with Manchester City into becoming City's longest-serving manager, spending 13 years in the dugout between 1950 and 1963. All in, that's a quarter of a century of service and well deserving of a page.

McDowall was the mastermind of the Revie plan, a system built around centre forward and future Leeds and England manager Don Revie, which helped City rise to the final of the FA Cup in 1954/55 (a loss to Newcastle United) and 1955/56 (a glorious victory against Birmingham City).

Towards the end of his time with the club, City were starting to find themselves propping up the table rather than leading it – the result of football moving on and the club finding itself slightly financially challenged and, therefore, unable to hold on to their best players. And so, after nearly a decade and a half at Maine Road, McDowall moved on.

THE OPPOSITION: MANCHESTER UNITED

Sibling rivalry or something more? Local derbies always have a certain extra something, and the matches between the two teams with Manchester in their name will always draw a crowd.

The teams first met formally in the FA Cup back in the Ardwick days of 1891. That first meeting wasn't necessarily anything to write home about, although anyone watching would have benefited from seeing five of the wrong sort of goals compared to one of the right sort, which broadly set the template for the next 115 and odd years.

To be fair, there have been seasons when Manchester City have been dominant, but up until the last decade and a half, it's United who have had the lion's share of the glory. Overall, City have won just under a third of the 189 matches that the two teams have played since 1891 in all competitions, while United have won a little over 40% of the time.

Focusing on the Premier League, it's fair to say it's been pretty much a game of two halves for both City and United. City have again won a little over a third of the time, while United have come away with the honours just under half the time. Since 2008 when City was taken over, things have been more evenly balanced in the top flight, with both sides winning just under 45% of the time.

Unsurprisingly, the 2011/12 season was the first time in the Premier League that City did the double over United, although they've repeated the feat in 2013/14, 2018/19 and 2021/22. If you hadn't heard the news, the good times are rolling.

No matter how the points fall, the crowds at a Manchester derby enjoy just under three goals a match on average, and there have been four or more goals around a quarter of the times that the two teams meet in the Premier League since 1992. At the other end of the scale, fewer than 10% of the matches have deflated into dispiriting goalless draws.

Basically, it's a complex psychology. There have been times when going up against United has felt a bit like

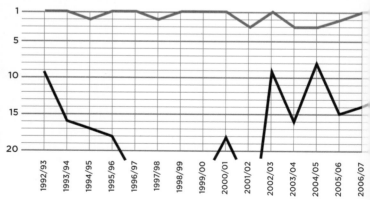

MANCHESTER CITY VERSUS MANCHESTER UNITED

David taking on Goliath, but the two teams are currently competing almost as equals, so it's probably fair to say that, on balance, football is generally the winner.

There's one big question to ask, though ... given what City have achieved over the last decade and comparing it to what United haven't, is it time to suggest that the sulky Salforders are no longer City's main rivals? That the better football, the better entertainment, has been on display when City face Liverpool, or even one of City's regular Champions League opponents?

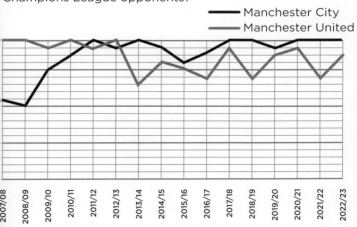

Manchester City
Manchester United

⭐ ALAN OAKES ⭐

Strikers are only as good as the balls that they are fed, and holding midfielder Alan Oakes was an exceptional provider of the ball. He joined Manchester City as an amateur in 1958, and was quickly thrust into the glamour of the era with duties that included cleaning Bert Trautmann's boots.

He signed on as a professional shortly afterwards, helping City through the difficult years of the early 1960s and then the glittering years as the decade wore on. He was part of the City set-up from 1959 to 1976, making 676 appearances in all competitions and finding the net 34 times.

He moved on from City to become player-manager at Third Division Chester, where he had the distinction of guiding them into the last 16 of the FA Cup, delivering victory in the Debenhams Cup (in the days when the Debenhams Cup, and, indeed, Debenhams, was a thing), nearly leading them into the Second Division, and giving Ian Rush his professional debut.

Oakes played alongside his cousin Glyn Pardoe at City, and both his son and his nephew went on to become professional footballers.

HUNTING FOR A ⋆ BRAND IDENTITY ⋆

Manchester City arose from humble beginnings as a football team based around a church in West Gorton. This means that when the team started out, they didn't have access to a team of branding gurus that could develop a visual identity for them, let alone actualise a workshop that would help them ideate the conceptual thrust behind the very notion of the team, its fans, and the city that it represents. No, they just sewed a simple white cross on to their black jerseys and then got on with playing football.

Despite this no-nonsense approach, it's worth noting that the cross the team used, technically known as the cross pattée (pronounced 'patty') pops up as a heraldic device throughout history. It has had various meanings but back in the days when it was being used by a small football team in the back streets of Manchester, it was likely to have been intended to reflect friendship, chivalry and honour.

It was also relatively simple to cut out and sew on to a football top, which is likely to have been relatively high on the list of reasons for adopting it. Either way, by the time that St Marks (West Gorton) metamorphosised into Ardwick, the cross pattée had been consigned to the history books.

In the late 1880s, the team were playing in a natty half dark blue/half light blue number, which then changed to half white/half light blue; however, by the time the 1890s rolled around, this had been simplified into a simple white top. The team had a badge – a quartered blue and white shield with the letters 'AAFC' (Ardwick Association Football Club) distributed one to a quarter – but none of the shirts of the time appear to have had a badge. Before shirt sponsorship it was probably more financially efficient to run out in an unadorned shirt.

★ NEIL YOUNG ★

Born and bred within half a mile of Maine Road, of course Neil Young would turn down an offer of joining Manchester United's apprentice scheme. It was City he wanted – and City he got.

He wasn't doing it for the glory. In 1962/63, his first full season, City were relegated to the Second Division, four points adrift of safety. City were sixth in the Second Division the year after, and 11th the year after that. But then, in 1965/66, it all started to go right: City were promoted as champions back to the top flight, and then made themselves champions of the First Division two years later.

This was the start of a period of unprecedented success, with the FA Cup in 1968/69 (with Young scoring the game's only goal), the Charity Shield in 1969 and then crowning it all with the Cup Winners' Cup in 1969/70.

He scored 86 goals in 334 league appearances for City, moving on to Preston North End and Rochdale as his playing days came to a close. People say that Young's achievements were often eclipsed by the exploits of Mike Summerbee, Francis Lee and Colin Bell (see pages 58, 64 and 68), and while you suspect that he wouldn't have had it any other way, it's important to acknowledge his contribution.

Four decades later, as City fought their way to another FA Cup win in 2011, and following a campaign by City supporters, thousands of fans raised scarfs in the iconic red and black to mark Young's contribution to the club. Proceeds from the sale of the scarves went to support Young and a local hospital in his final days.

BACK IN THE DAYS BEFORE ENTERTAINMENT BECAME A THING IN MANCHESTER, CITY SCORED A MERE 10 GOALS AT HOME FOR THE ENTIRETY OF THE 2006/07 SEASON. ANOTHER GREAT RECORD THAT NO ONE EVER WANTS TO ENDURE AGAIN.

"SOMEBODY WOULD GIVE HIM THE BALL AND I'D MAKE A RUN TO COLLECT IT IN THE BOX AND IT WOULD NEVER ARRIVE. I'D TURN AROUND AND HE'D BE JUGGLING IT LIKE A BLOODY SEAL,"

said Neil Young on Rodney Marsh. Was this the first time that someone suggested that Manchester City was a circus?

★ BLUE-SKY THINKING ★

The refinement of AAFC into Manchester City FC saw the team adopt a sky-blue shirt, white shorts and dark blue socks, and that was mostly how the home kit stayed for the next hundred years until City took on a slightly darker blue, technically called 'laser blue' at the time, for a brief period at the end of the 1990s.

To be fair, there were a few deviations before then. Sky-blue shirts and black shorts and socks were tried out for one season at the start of the 1890s, half black, half dark blue socks put in an appearance a few years later, and, in the psychedelic 1960s, City started to turn on, turn in and drop out by adding subtle burgundy accents to their socks. These accents have emerged once again in the 2022/23 kits – this time on the shirts. Could be a flashback to those heady days of late 1960s success?

City's badge also has a tendency of turning up in the middle of the chest rather than over the right breast, and away shirts have often been resplendent with a sash design. Although these are only a slight deviation from the norm, it's a sign of a team who are willing to do things slightly differently in a league full of teams that mostly all sing to the same tune.

THE RED AND BLACK AWAY KIT THAT WAS ADOPTED IN THE 1960S IS DIRECTLY INSPIRED BY AC MILAN. CITY WON THE FA CUP IN 1968/69, AND THEN BOTH THE LEAGUE CUP AND THE EUROPEAN CUP WINNERS' CUP IN 1970 WHILE WEARING RED AND BLACK, SO IT'S FAIR TO SAY THAT IT WORKED.

MIKE SUMMERBEE

Mike Summerbee spent a decade at Manchester City, adding swaggering attacks from the right wing to what is now the club's second most successful era. He made 449 appearances in a City shirt in all competitions, finding the net 67 times and offering numerous assists to the team.

His list of achievements as a City player is impressive. He helped get the team promoted as champions of the Second Division in his first season in 1965/66, and then helped win the First Division two seasons later. He helped bring the FA Cup to Maine Road in 1968/69, the League Cup in 1969/70, the Charity Shield in both 1968 and 1972, and the UEFA Cup Winners' Cup in 1969/70 (although injury kept him on the bench for the final, which at least kept him out of the torrential rain).

Summerbee also made eight appearances for England, scoring one goal, as the Three Lions rebuilt themselves after the 1966 World Cup victory.

He stayed local after his career at City came to an end, joining Blackpool (briefly) and Stockport County where he became player-manager.

BOUNDING WITH EFFORTLESS GRACE ACROSS THE WIDE MANCHESTER ★ SAVANNA ★

City have always had a tendency for doing things slightly differently, and in the case of the badge, this includes not really using one regularly on their playing shirts until the early 1970s, well after most teams had had been adorning themselves for a while.

Before this, when the team did use a badge, it was the full-blown coat of arms of the City of Manchester and its relatives and descendants (such as the Metropolitan District of the Greater Manchester County, the Greater Manchester Metropolitan County Council and the Greater Council of Greater Greater Manchester Councils which are Great), but there really isn't enough energy in the sun to delve into local councils, their remits and the crests that they deploy. The long and short of it is that the crest tended to come out for important matches like FA Cup finals (which City have graced 11 times, winning six so far).

While the crest only appeared on special occasions, it would be rude not to point out a couple of features. Firstly, the coat of arms was granted to Manchester in 1842. (The UK, you will be relieved to know, has an official authority for this kind of thing. It has an office and everything, because if everyone could just choose their own coat of arms willy-nilly, there would be anarchy. There would be lions rampant running rampant.)

The Manchester crest also has the three stripes that have put in frequent appearances on Manchester City's badge. They have come to represent the Irwell, the Irk and the Medlock, the three rivers that run through the city centre, but they originally came over from the coat of arms of former lords of the manor of Manchester, the de Gresles, who arrived in England with William the Conqueror in 1066. A few generations later, Magna Carta troublemaker Robert de Gresle had a simple red shield with three yellow stripes, technically known as 'three bendlets enhanced or' because, well, it just is. Whatever, the motif was carried through to the arrival of the Manchester coat of arms and from there on to City's modern badges.

Manchester's industrious bees also find their place on the city's coat of arms, distributed evenly around the world to reflect the role that the city played in the Industrial Revolution, taking goods to where they were needed.

Finally, honourable mention should go to the chap on the left of the coat of arms: that's not a unicorn, it's a far more down-to-earth antelope. Antelopes have been used in heraldic circles to exemplify harmony, leadership and peace, as well as purity and speed, since the days of Henry IV, Duke of Lancaster. The antelope on a coat of arms in Britain is basically a mythical beast rather than representing something that has roamed the plains of Lancashire in recent memory. They might have had them over the Pennine hills in Yorkshire, but no one can find a train that works to go over and find out.

Sorry, a book about football, you say ...

"WE WILL WIN THE EUROPEAN CUP. EUROPEAN FOOTBALL IS FULL OF COWARDS AND WE'LL TERRORISE THEM."

The problem is that European football wasn't and Manchester City didn't, but you can't fault Malcolm Allison's confidence as he took Manchester City to Europe in the early 1970s. Perhaps he was just ahead of this time.

★ FRANCIS LEE ★

Francis Lee has led what can safely be called a full and rich life. Lancashire-born, he enjoyed an eight-year footballing apprenticeship at Bolton Wanderers, before joining Manchester City in 1967 for what was then a club record transfer fee of £60,000. Yes, there was a time, just 60 years ago, when you could count the number of zeros on the fingers hand.

He joined a City team that already boasted the talents ofNeil Young, Mike Summerbee and Colin Bell (see pages 54, 60 and 66), and together they delighted Maine Road and delivered five years of unprecedented success. He made 249 league appearances for City, knocking in 112 goals, and was the team's top or joint top scorer for five consecutive years. He pulled on an England shirt 27 times, finding the back of the net 10 times.

He left City for Derby in 1974, and while he didn't want the move, a second Division One winners' medal followed, which presumably sweetened the pill somewhat.

After hanging up his boots he became a respected racehorse trainer and enjoyed a successful business career, at one point employing comedian Peter Kay in one of his toilet paper factories. He took control of City in the mid-1990s, spending four years as chairman.

·MANCHESTER CITY·

Season	Player	Goals
2002/03	Nicolas Anelka	14
2003/04	Nicolas Anelka	16
2004/05	Robbie Fowler	11
2005/06	Andrew Cole	9
2006/07	Joey Barton	6
2007/08	Elano	8
2008/09	Robinho	14
2009/10	Carlos Tevez	23
2010/11	Carlos Tevez	20
2011/12	Sergio Agüero	23
2012/13	Edin Džeko	14
2013/14	Yaya Touré	20
2014/15	Sergio Agüero	26
2015/16	Sergio Agüero	24
2016/17	Sergio Agüero	20
2017/18	Sergio Agüero	21
2018/19	Sergio Agüero	21
2019/20	Raheem Sterling	20
2020/21	Ilkay Gündoğan	13
2021/22	Kevin De Bruyne	15
2022/23	Erling Haaland	36

Goals 0 5 10

MAN CITY'S LEADING GOAL SCORERS BY ★ SEASON ★

(PREMIER LEAGUE)

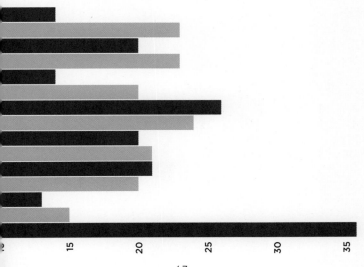

★ COLIN BELL ★

Colin Bell was a humble man with a number of names. They called him 'the King of the Kippax' as his midfield exploits gave Maine Road's most vocal stand so many things to sing about. He was also known as 'Nijinsky' after a famous racehorse that was renowned for its stamina.

Bell joined Manchester City in the Second Division midway through the 1965/66 season from Bury, where he'd had an impressive three seasons. His arrival at Maine Road galvanised the squad, and City clinched the title in 1967/68 for the first time since the 1936/37 season. He also helped the team win the Charity Shield and League Cup twice, as well as the FA Cup and the European Cup Winners' Cup.

He made 498 appearances for City in total, scoring 153 times, and he also earned 48 England caps, scoring nine times.

He stayed with City until 1979, although his last few years were blighted by a knee injury that seriously hampered his performances. He then briefly joined former Manchester United rival George Best at the San Jose Earthquakes in the US league, before returning to City as a youth and reserve team coach.

★ CROSSING THE DIVIDE ★

For two teams with such a strong geographical and fraternal bond, the destinies of Manchester City and Manchester United have never really been very closely linked. There are a fair few players who have played for both teams, though, and sometimes the result has been legendary. Sometimes, however, it's been less impressive ...

Let's start with the slightly weird: The early days of football were quite a long time ago, and some of the paperwork has got lost between then and now, but it appears that Horace Blew, a Wrexham-born full-back played a single game for Manchester United towards the end of the 1905/06 season. He then moved on to Manchester City. Where he played a single game at the start of the 1906/07 season. His opinion about being the only player to turn out once for both City and United is also lost to history.

More recently, there was, of course, Denis Law – a stalwart of United during the 1960s who also had two stints with City. Virtually his last kick of the ball as a professional footballer was aptly in a Manchester derby at the tail end of the 1973/74 season. It was a sublimely cheeky back heel that found the back of the net and quashed United's dim hopes of avoiding relegation ... For the record, results elsewhere meant that United had already been relegated into the Second Division, but Law didn't know that at the time.

Back at the dawn of time, Billy Meredith was one of football's first superstars. He signed for City in 1894, making 338 league appearances before being charged with match fixing and banned from playing for 18 months at the end of the 1904/05 season. He signed for United in 2006, where he stayed for 15 war-interrupted years (he may have won some trophies, but it was with United so they don't really count). He came back to City in 1921 at the ripe old age of 47, where he spent the last three years of his career, making a further 28 league appearances.

Another player involved with the 1905 match-fixing incident who then went on to join United was Sandy Turnbull. He was also banned from playing for City and moved down the road, along with Jimmy Bannister, Herbert Burgess and Billy Meredith. In 1915, he was at the centre of another match-fixing scandal, this time between United and Liverpool, which ultimately knocked on to become one of the foundations of the whole issue between Tottenham and Arsenal. But that's a whole other story, and not one that needs concern us here …

Then, of course, there's the Great Dane himself, Peter Schmeichel (who is half Polish by birth, but never let the facts get in the way of a good nickname), who obviously had a legendary eight-year career with United before leaving in 1999. He moved on but three years later realised that Manchester is the bright centre of the universe and joined City for a year, giving him the opportunity to become the only person to have played for both sides of the city and never been on the losing side of a derby match.

Honourable mention should also go to Alec Herd (see page 28) and his son, David. Alec played for City for the best part of 15 years, making 257 league appearances between 1933 and 1948. His son, loyal to greater Manchester at least, turned out for United between 1961 and 1968. Sweetly, the pair played together at Stockport County while Alec was in the twilight of his career and David was coming up through the ranks.

Keeping it in the family, there are also Matthew and Billy Gillespie, two Scottish brothers who lined up against one another in the Manchester derbies of the late 19th and early 20th centuries.

All right, if we are being picky, neither of the Herd or the Gillespie boys actually pulled on the blue shirt and then the red shirt or vice versa, but surely any time two brothers face each other or a father and child end up playing on the same team, this should be acknowledged, even if it's somewhat tangential to the matter at hand ...

So, obviously, the final word should go to Carlos Tevez, whose move from United to City in 2009 showed how serious the rejuvenated City intended to be. Tevez had formed an exceptional strike partnership with Cristiano Ronaldo and Wayne Rooney during his loan period with United, but he left the Salford-based club to come to Manchester proper and played for City for four years, making 113 league appearances and scoring 58 league goals.

KEEPING IT SIMPLE

Liverpool also used to use their city's crest as their badge for the first 50 years of their existence – until some bright spark on the city council pointed out, in the 1950s, that they weren't the only team in the city, and perhaps they should not assume that they played for the whole city.

Manchester City is the only major professional team that plays in the city of Manchester, but by the 1960s it became clear that plain shirts weren't going to cut it any more. So, in 1965, the team developed a new badge, which started to be added to their shirts on a full-time basis in the early 1970s.

The first badge was fairly simple. It kept the central shield of the city crest, complete with the three stripes and the ship at sea and put it in a circle with the words Manchester City F.C. written around the edges. It was simple, it was eye catching ... there might have been a few too many dots on it if we were being picky, but it more than did the job.

In 1972, the colouring evolved and the three stripes in the shield were replaced with a red rose of Lancashire, but after that there were only tweaks for the next quarter of a century.

LES MCDOWALL ORIGINALLY TRAINED AS A DRAUGHTSMAN (SOMEONE WHO MADE TECHNICAL PLANS OR DRAWINGS BACK IN THE DAYS BEFORE COMPUTERS WERE A THING), BUT DURING AN ECONOMIC DOWNTURN HE FOUND HIMSELF WITHOUT A JOB. AN INDUSTRIOUS FELLOW, HE FORMED A FOOTBALL TEAM TO KEEP HIMSELF OCCUPIED BETWEEN INTERVIEWS, GOT SPOTTED BY A SCOUT FOR SUNDERLAND, WAS OFFERED PROFESSIONAL TERMS – AND NEVER LOOKED BACK.

★ TOMMY BOOTH ★

Football is a form of entertainment, so all eyes are usually on the midfielders and strikers as they strive to get the ball forward, get past a defence and find the back of the net. But what gives them the confidence to swash their buckles and make their runs? Having a solid, well-organised defence that they can rely on.

If they are very lucky, that defence will include Tommy Booth, who quietly gave Manchester City the foundation to build on through thick and thin from 1967 to 1981. Defensive maestro he may have been, but he also turned in more than his share of goals, including a last gasp wallop off a corner in the final moments of the 1968/69 FA Cup semi-final that saw off Everton and got City to the final. Booth then helped City's defence keep a clean sheet in the final while Neil Young got the goal that gave City the cup.

Booth joined City in 1965 as a youth player, turning professional two years later. He made 487 first team appearances for City over 16 years, delivering 36 goals along the way. He helped City win the FA Cup, the European Cup Winners' Cup and the League Cup twice.

Towards the end of his playing days Booth joined Preston North End, spending three years there before retiring due to injury.

★ JOE CORRIGAN ★

Sale-born Joe Corrigan, known as 'Big Joe' on account of being 193 cm in his socks (6 foot 4 inches), stood between the sticks for Manchester City between 1967 and 1983. He made 602 appearances in all competitions.

Like most players who stuck with City for a long time, Corrigan enjoyed good times and suffered the bad. In the aftermath of the exceptional team of the late 1960s, City stumbled into mid-table obscurity during the 1970s, recovered in the middle of the decade and then went into a slow, dull decline into relegation in the 1982/83 season.

But 20th-century City was never for the faint of heart, and Corrigan was clearly full of heart. In the midst of the decline, though, City still managed to reach the final of the centenary FA Cup in 1980/81, playing against Tottenham Hotspur. The game ended up going to a replay after an unfortunate own goal levelled the score in extra time in the first leg. Spurs (somehow) won the replay, but Corrigan was named man of the match for both matches. Given the choice, they probably aren't the trophies he would have wanted to win, but he deserved them nonetheless.

Corrigan was capped nine times for England, a number that would probably have been higher if he hadn't been playing during the era of Peter Shilton (who received 125 caps between 1970 and 1990) and Ray Clemence (who received 61 caps between 1972 and 1983). Corrigan took it in his mighty stride, though, pointing out that he would have been honoured to win even a single cap.

Corrigan continued to be a presence in the game after his professional career came to an end, working as a goalkeeping coach for several clubs. He has continued to be a regular presence at the Etihad.

MANCHESTER CITY SCORED 104 GOALS IN 1957/58, ONLY TO CONCEDE 100 GOALS IN THE SAME SEASON. THE SEASON'S CHAMPIONS, WOLVERHAMPTON WANDERERS, SCORED 103 GOALS BUT ONLY CONCEDED 47.

"IF ANYONE ASKS ME IF I WOULD HAVE LIKED TO PLAY TODAY, I SAY 'NO, I HAD A FABULOUS CAREER, I MET SOME GREAT PEOPLE AND A FEW VILLAINS BUT I WOULD NOT CHANGE MY CAREER FOR ALL THE TEA IN CHINA."

Joe Corrigan doesn't look back in anger.

THE LOGO THAT MADE
★ YOU ASK, "WHY?" ★

In 1997, with the rumblings of a copyright challenge in the background, the leadership at Manchester City felt that it was a good time for a change of badge. And so, out of the clear blue skies, an eagle landed on the chests of the Manchester City players, accompanied by three eyebrow-raising golden stars. Out went the blooming rose of Lancashire and back came Norman aristocratic/three river stripes – this time white on blue.

It's fair to say that some people had opinions about the new logo. Some suggested that the eagle looked more like a chicken. Others asked why there were three stars above the badge when most clubs only added a single star to their badge for each time they'd achieved European glory.

Most agreed, though, that the badge had a lot going on and, while much of it may be theoretically quite cool, only the central section really reflected the heritage of

Manchester City. Generally, it was not all that popular. They stuck with it for two decades, but in 2015 City decided to consult the fans about where they wanted the logo to go next.

And the resounding answer was that the fans would please like to go back to the old round logo, slightly updated to reflect modern design sensibilities, thank you. This time around the three stripes survived the change, tastefully present in the background behind a resplendent red rose of Lancashire, satisfying fans of both the 1960s and 1970s version of the logo.

The badge read simply 'Manchester City', rather than 'Manchester City F.C.', putting the word 'Manchester' at the top and the word 'City' at the bottom, which did away with all those pesky dots that made people feel so subconsciously irritable whenever they'd looked at the older versions of the logo. Highlighting the club's heritage, the year 1894 was also added across the middle, reflecting the year that the club became Manchester City. Simple, effective and now fully copyright-protected.

• MANCHESTER CITY •

JOE MERCER

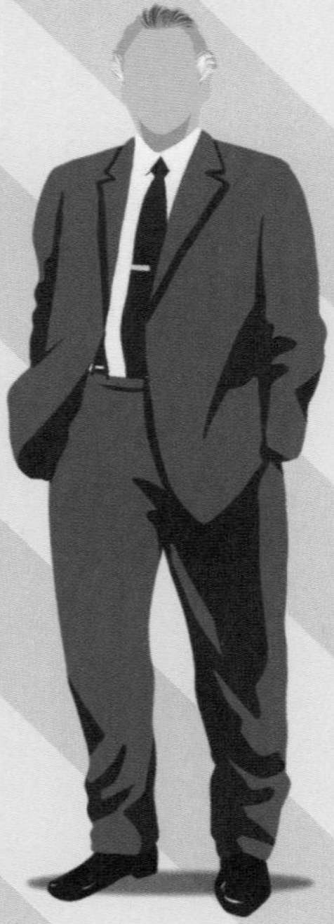

Joe Mercer was the captain of Arsenal's decorated post-World War II team. He was an Evertonian by birth (and played for the Toffees) and his father played for Nottingham Forest and Tranmere Rovers. None of this should be held against him because, between 1965 and 1971, Mercer, ably assisted by Malcolm Allison, led Manchester City out of the Second Division to the top of the First Division, hunted down both the FA and League Cups and made City the champions of Europe. In the torrential rain that Manchester took with them to Vienna.

Mercer also enjoyed a successful spell as caretaker England manager, leading the team to joint victory in the British Home Championship in 1974, which, to be fair to it, had been around for 90 years at that point and was in no way a consolation prize for the Three Lions' (as well as the Welsh and Northern Irish) failure to get through to the World Cup finals.

The team he built at City in the mid- to late-1960s is still talked about with reverence and, with the exception of the League Cup in 1975/76, was the last time that City tasted glory for three and a half decades.

MANCHESTER CITY WOMEN'S FOOTBALL
★ CLUB ★

Manchester City Ladies FC was one of the first women's teams to be directly affiliated with a professional football club in the north-west of England. They started out at the end of 1988 as a community initiative that was built out of a five-a-side tournament. City discussed the possibility of setting up a standing women's squad and were impressed when a lot of potential players turned up for trials.

The team enjoyed the active support of both the wider City hierarchy and the women's FA, but the struggles of the men's team as the 1990s progressed had an impact on the women's team's ambitions.

Women's football in England was reorganised in 2010 with the formation of the Women's Super League (WSL). The inaugural season was in 2011, but it was three years before the newly renamed Manchester City Women's Football Club joined the league. Based on their affiliation with one of the largest men's teams in the world and an array of talent that they had attracted to the club, City's women's team came straight into the top flight, achieving a creditable fifth out of eight teams.

The year after saw things get into gear. A run of 10 matches unbeaten helped City to second place in the league and provided qualification for the Champion's League. A year later they went one better and were crowned champions of the WSL.

With competition getting ever fiercer and crowds continuing to rise, City have been second in the WSL in four of the last five years. The one year that they missed out on second (in 2021/22), they came third. There has also been success in the FA Cup and League Cup, and fourth in the very competitive 2022/23 season is not to be sniffed at.

With the recent victory in the Euros, it seems likely that the women's game has reached a level of momentum that should mean teams are viewed in their own right rather than being seen as an additional part of the activities of the men's club. The Euros final sold out Wembley, and while some of that will have been driven by the fact that it was the host nation taking on a long-term nemesis, a recent Manchester derby attracted a crowd of nearly 45,000, suggesting that there's a healthy appetite for the women's game.

IN THE 1925/26 SEASON, CITY BECOME THE FIRST MANCHESTER TEAM TO PLAY AT WEMBLEY AS THEY BECAME RUNNERS-UP IN THE FA CUP. THEY ALSO RECORDED A 6-1 WIN OVER MANCHESTER UNITED AT OLD TRAFFORD, THE BIGGEST VICTORY IN THE DERBY TO THIS DAY. THEY WERE ALSO RELEGATED.

"YOU'VE GOT THE PROSPECT OF WINNING THE FIRST EVER DOMESTIC TREBLE IN THIS COUNTRY..."

(reporter ahead of men's 2019 FA Cup final)

"THE FIRST TIME FOR THE MEN. THE WOMEN HAVE WON IT."

Pep Guardiola, a man with both focus and perspective.

THE OPPOSITION:
★ TOTTENHAM HOTSPUR ★

Tottenham Hotspur have had a habit of being Spursy since before anyone can remember. They often bring through teams with impressive players that seem to play well together, but then ... never ... quite ... But they also never collapse in a heap either. They are just always there, mostly striving for a Champions League place, a team you need to get past when you are hunting for glory.

To be fair, they did successfully stand in City's way in

the 1980/81 FA Cup final, when a 1–1 draw led to a replay and 3–2 defeat for City (a fabulous volley by City's Steve McKenzie and Kevin Reeves' calmly taken penalty just weren't enough). They also beat City to take the final Champions League place at the end of the 2009/10 season when the two teams were both vying for a trip to Europe, Spurs for the first time, City for the first time since the glorious, victorious 1969/70 campaign. And there was also the incident in the 2018/19 Champions League semi-finals when Tottenham went through on away goals ... beyond that, though, there's not much that you might call a legendary rivalry.

The two teams have played 168 times in all competitions since they first faced each other in 1909, and in the century and a bit in between, honours have been even, with both City and Spurs winning around 40% of the time (draws making up the balance).

Like pretty much all of City's opposition teams, the Premier League has been a game of two halves: first half bad, second half good from City's perspective. Beyond that, there's not too much worth drawing out.

That could all change, though. There's always next year with Tottenham.

•MANCHESTER CITY•

PAUL LAKE

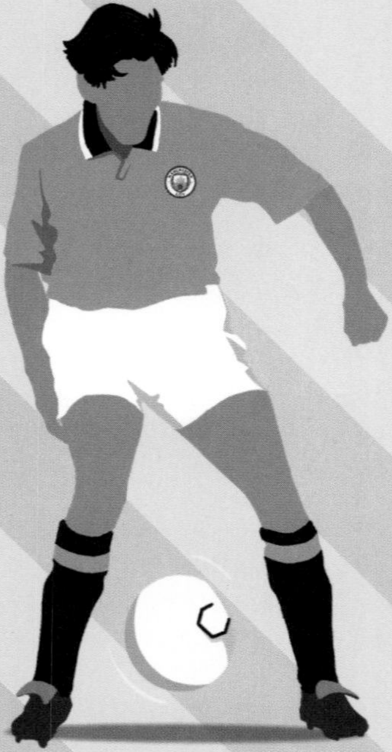

Football can be truly heartbreaking. Millions of kids all around the world start playing when they are very young, heads full of dreams of what it would be like to score a winning goal at the Etihad, Wembley or some of the other places where football is allegedly played.

Some of them have the skills to catch the eye of a scout, and a handful of them put in the hard work, have the support and are willing to make the sacrifices that are necessary to become a professional footballer.

One of this small number was Paul Lake, who worked with the Manchester City youth set-up throughout his teens and signed on as a professional on his 18th birthday in 1986. A defender and midfielder, he scored on his home debut and became a regular first team player over the next couple of seasons, helping City get back into the First Division at the end of the 1988/89 season. He became club captain in 1990/91.

All this work, all this potential, was lost when a ruptured anterior cruciate ligament essentially ended his career at the age of 23. He played for City 110 times in the First Division and the Premier League, scoring seven goals. He retrained as a physiotherapist and is still involved in the football industry.

THREE KITS TO
★ THE WIND ★

People will moan about anything – they always have and
they always will. One of the things that people like to
moan about is football kits: there are too many of them,
and they are too expensive. "Why should I fork out £65
for a first kit, £65 for a second kit and £65 for a third kit?"
they rage in the duller corners of the internet.

The standard response is that unless you are the parent of
a player, you don't need to fork out for all three kits, and, if
truth be known, most clubs probably let their players have
their kits for free. (Although rumour has it that Tottenham
players have to iron their own names on to the backs of
their shirts. And darn their own socks.)

These days, though, a club that is fighting in four
competitions needs at least three kits because you can't
create a shirt that will be different enough to every other
team in the top two flights of Europe and the top four
leagues in England. Fans don't like massive changes to

their primary kits unless it's a very special year. So, the collars may change, there might be a flourish here and there, but basically the first team kit has to be consistent to avoid upsetting the fans.

Which means that it's the second and third kits where the designers can have some fun.

Manchester City have always had a strong affiliation with Manchester's thriving design scene, which most recently tends to come out in the third shirts, although the away kits can sometimes bring in more innovative/ wayward design elements. The kinds of things that might be more familiar on a 1980s goalie strip rather than the shirt of your modern outfield player.

There are some things that have come to echo down the generations. The sash that sometimes appears on City's away strips has a half-century heritage, while the red and black stripes have been around even longer, after coach Malcom Allison decided to try to borrow a little bit of AC Milan's European panache and use a similar colour scheme from 1968. Homage or appropriation? Either way, it's worth noting that City lost the first couple of games in the strip, which goes to show that it's not just legendary players that can have a rocky start.

Some people like something a little different and, in the end, designers deserve to have a little fun. Care needs to be taken though, with City getting unfavourable headlines for their 2019/20 second kit and the 2020/21 third kit. In the case of the 2019/20 kit, the black and yellow stripes on the shoulders were intended to echo legendary Manchester nightclub the Haçienda, which featured similar chevrons on its pillars. Unfortunately, the Haçienda's interior designer was put out that the team behind the City kit hadn't consulted him and the media made merry. The 2020/21 third kit, meanwhile, was a paisley affair that was supposed to evoke the 1960's glory days of Manchester City and the late 1980's splendour of the Madchester scene. Not many people were mad for it.

Still, though, it's about time the royal blue/neon yellow striped away kit from the 1998/99 season made a comeback.

"SILKY SMOOTH FIZZY BUBBLECH MCFC."

Enigmatic City fan Liam Gallagher took to Twitter with just the right words to describe City's performances as the 2022/23 season drew to a close.

★ PAUL DICKOV ★

Watching Paul Dickov was one of the few bright things about being a Manchester City supporter in the 1990s. 'Chaos' is not a big enough word to describe quite what was going on at the club during his first spell there. Without dwelling on it too much, he worked with five managers during his first season at City, and, yes, two of those managers were caretakers – but that much chopping and changing in the dugout is not what you might call conducive to a positive footballing experience for players or fans. Just ask Chelsea.

Dickov played 131 times for City in all competitions, scoring 41 goals over two spells with the club from 1996 to 2002 and then 2006 to 2008. He also played 10 times for Scotland, scoring once.

In the end, who can forget his injury-time equaliser in the Second Division play-off final against Gillingham at Wembley? That'll teach people to try to leave early. Them were the days ...

THE OPPOSITION: ★ ARSENAL ★

Up until recently, there's never really been much beef between Manchester City and Arsenal. They've played each other competitively in various forms since they first met back in the Second Division in 1893 (the Gunners won), but the great teams haven't tended to coincide with each other, so it's tended to be a fairly transactional relationship for most of their joint history.

They've faced each other 208 times in all competitions, and it's generally best to draw a veil over the specific statistics up until 2008.

Drilling down into the Premier League and ... yeah, to be fair, it's much the same ...

The good news is that since 2008, City have been in the ascendency and Arsenal have, to put it bluntly, been mostly heading in the opposite direction, so the data offers the following slightly startling statistics ...

Prior to the 2008/09 season, City had won just 5% of Premier League matches against Arsenal. Since the 2008/09 season, City have won 60% of their Premier League matches against Arsenal. City have also won the last 12 Premier League meetings between the two teams.

Arsenal very kindly kept the throne at the top of the Premier League warm for Manchester City for most of the 2022/23 season. The only time you really have to be at the top is at the end of May though, and that, for the third consecutive season and the fifth time in six seasons, is exactly where City put themselves.

Player	Club
Michael Owen	Liverpool, Newcastle United, Manchester United, Stoke City
Jermain Defoe	Bournemouth, Sunderland, Tottenham Hotspur, Portsmouth, West Ham, Charlton Athletic
Robbie Fowler	Liverpool, Leeds, Manchester City, Blackburn Rovers
Thierry Henry	Arsenal
Frank Lampard	West Ham, Chelsea, Manchester City
Sergio Agüero	Manchester City
Andrew Cole	Sunderland, Portsmouth, Manchester City, Fulham, Blackburn Rovers, Manchester United, Newcastle United
Wayne Rooney	Everton, Manchester United
Harry Kane	Tottenham Hotspur
Alan Shearer	Blackburn Rovers, Newcastle United

Goals

PREMIER LEAGUE'S
★ TOP SCORERS ★

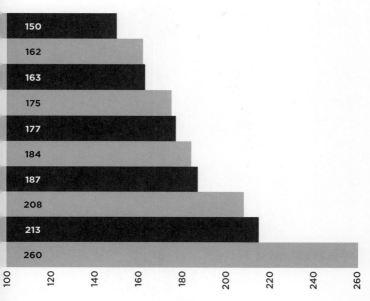

150
162
163
175
177
184
187
208
213
260

100 120 140 160 180 200 220 240 260

★ SHAUN GOATER ★

Shaun Goater originally came to the English leagues via Manchester United. He joined Rotherham United in 1989 to gain playing experience, stayed there for the best part of seven years, went to Notts County on loan for a single match and then spent a couple of years at Bristol City, before finally starting his career as a footballer in 1998 by joining Manchester City.

Even by City standards, these were difficult times, with the club in the process of being relegated to the third tier of English football for the first time in its history. Goater didn't stop, though, knocking in 21 of City's 33 goals as the team resurrected itself, via the play-offs, into the First Division in the 1998/99 season. He was City's top scorer again a year later, delivering 29 goals as City secured back-to-back promotions and reached the Premier League. The year after was not so good, with City dropping back down, despite Goater's 11 goals making him the top scorer for the third successive season.

He was also the top scorer for the fourth time in the 2001/02 season, finding the net more than 30 times as City were promoted back to the Premier League.

He made a total of 212 appearances' for City, scoring 103

goals, the 100th and 101st of which were in the 3–1 victory in the final Manchester derby to be played at Maine Road. He later said that his celebration was muted during the match because he'd noticed plenty of other teams getting caught out by over-celebrating goals against United and getting caught back, and he didn't want City going the same way.

Goater played several times for his native Bermuda and now works as a coach. It's probably fair to say that he got to see more English stadiums during his time with City than he would if he'd played for any other club.

FORMER CITY PLAYER SANDY TURNBULL WAS THE FIRST PERSON TO BE SENT OFF IN A MANCHESTER DERBY. HE WAS PLAYING FOR UNITED AT THE TIME THOUGH.

"I WALKED IN AND HE SAID 'SHAUN, HOW ARE YOU?'. I SAID: 'I'M REALLY LACKING IN CONFIDENCE' AND I HEARD HIM SAYING BACK: 'YES, YOU ARE RUBBISH.'"

Shaun Goater went to see a sports psychologist who was also a City fan after his first unsuccessful season at City. Whatever the psychologist said clearly worked though.

THE OPPOSITION:
★ LIVERPOOL ★

Manchester City and Liverpool have faced each other 223 times in all competitions – a number that rises by precisely one if you take the Ardwick days into account. That meeting took place early in the 1893/94 season at Hyde Park in the Second Division, but it was a decade and 10 matches before City found the key to beating the Reds.

Victories were few and far between for the first century or so, with Liverpool taking glory in just under half of the meetings between the two teams, a proportion that remained for the first 15 years of the Premier League.

Since 2008, though, things have been a lot more evenly balanced, with City now winning just under a third of the time, the two teams drawing a little more than a third of the time, and City doing the other thing around a third of the time.

And this is probably at the heart of the current tensions between City and Liverpool: for the last decade, more often than not it's been these two teams that have been vying for the title and scrapping it out for trophies. Both teams have boasted exceptional talent on the pitch, and both have enjoyed the services of managers who are fierce competitors but also, seemingly, decent blokes. It's meant that when the Premier League fixtures are announced, checking the date of the match in Salford has become less interesting than checking the date of the trip along the M62.

It's worth remembering that Pep Guardiola and Jürgen Klopp faced each other eight times in the two years they were managing Bayern Munich and Borussia Dortmund respectively – a match that is known in Bundesliga circles as *Der Klassiker* (online translation services are available). Honours were split in the two team's meetings, with each winning four times.

Back in the real world, City and Liverpool have faced each other 30 times since 2008, and only two of those meetings have ended in scoreless draws. Sticking with the rule of thirds, if you are lucky enough to get tickets to a Premier League match between City and Liverpool, there's a decent chance of a spectacle, with three or more goals around a third of the time.

Ultimately, you can talk about the history of the two cities, how the ship canal changed economic fortunes, and so on and so forth, but the reality is that the rivalry between the two football teams is basically less than a decade old. It was forged in the heat of Premier League title races, with the two teams taking first and second position in three of the last five years and jointly taking 50% of the top four positions in every year since 2016/17.

The bottom line is that whenever City faces Liverpool it's a fiercely contested match, and football's the real winner.

"IF YOU WERE A RACEHORSE, THEY'D SHOOT YOU."

Francis Lee to 37-year-old Mike Summerbee. The pair enjoyed an honest working relationship.

• MANCHESTER CITY •

JILL SCOTT

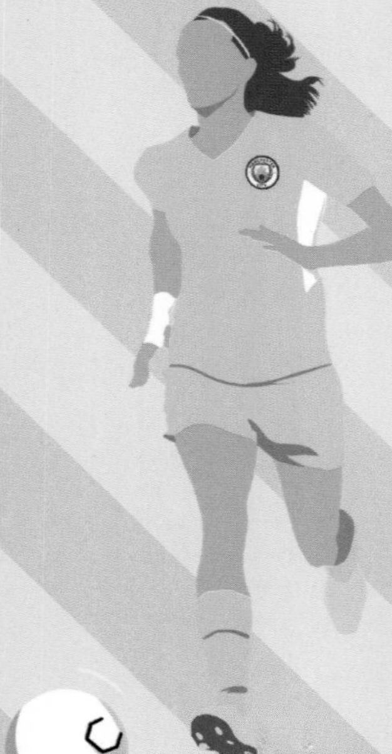

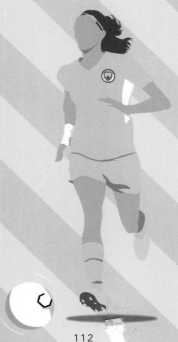

Jill Scott enjoyed a successful, storied career at the centre of women's football as it emerged from a niche hobby to become an important part of Britain's sporting heritage and a fixture of the television schedules.

Scott started out in her native Sunderland and spent seven years at Everton, where she helped them win the FA Women's Premier League Cup in 2007/08 and the FA Women's Cup in 2009/10.

In 2013, she joined Manchester City, and went on to make 111 league appearances, delivering 19 goals, over the course of her nine years with the club (although the final two seasons were predominantly spent out on loan, initially back with Everton and finally with Aston Villa).

The right-footed midfielder has also become an icon for England. Her 161 caps gives her the second highest number of appearances for the lionesses (after Fara Williams' 172 caps), and she was a key component of the team that won the UEFA Women's Euro 2022. She also made nine appearances for Great Britain teams at the 2012 and 2020 Tokyo Olympics.

Despite saying that she felt a fair amount of imposter syndrome, Scott marked her retirement by winning the

2022 series of *I'm a Celebrity ... Get Me Out of Here!*

You can argue about whether the rise of women's football in the public consciousness is the result of an exceptional run by the women's team in recent years or the fact that the broadcasting rights are significantly cheaper than the men's equivalent. The long and the short of it, though, is if there wasn't an audience, women's football wouldn't end up on telly – and you don't get on, let alone win, *I'm a Celebrity* unless you've got a certain national credibility. She became 'Queen of the Jungle' by beating some bloke off *Hollyoaks* and a former member of Boris Johnson's Big Laughs Party. How much more credible can you get?

"I SAW A LOAD OF BOYS PLAYING IN THE SCHOOL YARD AND I WALKED STRAIGHT UP TO THEM AND SAID THE FOUR MAGIC WORDS ... 'CAN I PLAY TOO?'"

Jill Scott on how she got started on the game. Could she play? Yes, she really could.

★ THE WHAT IFS ... ★

City has enjoyed an unprecedented period of success over the last decade and a half, with each of the last three managers delivering a title and numerous trophies (Brian Kidd was a caretaker so doesn't really count). City also won the top flight under Wilf Wild in the 1936/37 season and Joe Mercer in 1967/68, but it's also worth acknowledging the other managers that got City close to, but not quite over, the line.

In 1903/04, Tom Maley's tactical nous and application of what was known as the Scottish style of passing football took City to within four points of winning the league in the same season as bringing the FA Cup to Hyde Road. The club might well have delivered the first English double that year if they hadn't been victim of fixture congestion at the end of the season and been forced to play five games in a little over two weeks. It is likely the club would have been challenging for the top spot again a year later if there hadn't been a dispute with the FA over payments to players that led to the team being dismantled.

A decade and a half later, in 1920/21, Ernest Mangnall, the only person in the history of football to manage both City and Manchester United, led City to within five points of coming joint top. At the time it was only two points for a win, so five points was more of a gap than it would be today. And, credit where credit's due, the season's winners, Burnley, had a phenomenal goal average which would have given them the title even if City had tied with them on points.

Finally, in the 1976/77 season, there is one of those moments in history that makes you wonder what would have happened if City had taken just two more points and overtaken Liverpool to win the league. Just one more victory under Tony Book and the pain of the 1980s and 1990s could have been completely different ... Perhaps, but Derby County won the league in 1974/75 and they ended up bobbing up and down between the leagues alongside City throughout the following decades.

Winning the league might have changed everything, but then again, it might not ...

★ DAVID SILVA ★

David Silva spent a decade at Manchester City, making 436 appearances and providing 77 goals in all competitions. In the league, he made 309 appearances, scoring 60 times but also delivering 92 assists as he played his advanced midfield maestro role just behind the striker to a tee. (Technically, he tended to play as what is known as a *trequartista*, but how detailed are you expecting this book to be?)

Silva came through the Valencia youth system (where his father was responsible for stadium safety) before joining City at the start of the 2010/11 season. He adjusted to the rigours of the Premier League quickly, and helped the team become champions for the first time a year later. In total, he helped City win the Premier League four times, the FA Cup twice, the League Cup five times and the Community Shield three times.

Away from City, Silva won three consecutive international titles with Spain: the European Championship in 2008, the World Cup in 2010 and a second European Championship in 2012. In total, he won 125 caps for his country.

THE TROUBLE ★ WITH TREBLES ★

Winning the Premier League is thought to be directly worth around £44 million in prize money. Champions League glory brings in around £64 million when you take into account the contribution you get for winning each stage of the campaign, while a win in the FA Cup brings £2 million with an additional potential £1.3 million in winnings on your way to the final.

What this means is that a history-making, treble-winning team that's hoovered up nearly every scintilla of glory that's available, earns its club around £110 million.

Now, £110 million is not to be sniffed at. And in a phenomenal treble-winning year, demand for tickets to see the team play will increase, you'll also sell a lot more replica shirts, and doing well always delivers a range of revenue-enhancing opportunities.

The trouble is that to win the treble, a team needs to have

serious depth to its squad, which is not something that comes cheap. The going rate for a world-class, game-changing striker is now getting on for £100 million, and a team that wants to contest for the treble probably needs at least three players of that calibre.

There's also the transport to think about. With the return of inflation, a whole range of economic woes and increasing awareness of the environmental implications, you can't fly as cheaply as you did five years ago. That said, you can get a flight from Manchester to Madrid on a Monday afternoon, coming back on a Wednesday morning, for around £170, including two nights in a reasonably priced hotel. But that doesn't even include breakfast. Add in food and, even if your players were okay with a sandwich from the newsagent at the airport, you are not going to see much change from £300 per head for a European adventure. And a Premier League team that is off to Europe in search of glory is likely to need to take a team and an entourage that could stretch to 100 people, so that's £30,000 for a single match.

But even then it's not that simple. This may come as a shock, but many of the players on your modern treble-challenging football team are unlikely to be satisfied with a budget flight, a cheese and mystery meat airport sandwich and a shared room in a competitively priced hotel. The reality is that you can probably at least triple the £30,000 cost of a round without even blinking. And there are 10 rounds of the Champion's League if you start in the group stage.

Obviously, the domestic competitions are cheaper to get to and from, but the long and the short of it is that £110 million of prize money is not actually very much in the scheme of things, and the odds of winning a treble, even for the very best teams, are very, very slim.

But what about the even more elusive quadruple? There are two points to make here.

Firstly, the FA Community Shield adds a never unwelcome £1.25 million but, let's be honest, £1.25 million isn't much considering everthing. The alternative is the League Cup, but this only offers £100,000 to the winning team, which is not even enough to put the 'Haa' in Haaland. This is why people tend to talk about the domestic treble in a smaller font.

Secondly, the quadruple in any formation doesn't lend itself to simple chapter headings that will have brought a smile to the faces of the five sci-fi fans that have accidentally stumbled into this book.

The odds of winning the treble are infinitesimally small, and while the financial rewards might look big, it's amazing how quickly a bucket load of cash evaporates.

In the end though, very few of us are in football for the money. Most of us are here for the fun, the community, and, when it comes along, the glory.

And how glorious was June 10, 2023?

ON 12 NOVEMBER 1881, ST MARK'S (WEST GORTON) – WHO EVOLVED INTO MANCHESTER CITY – HOSTED NEWTON HEATH LYR – WHO EVOLVED INTO MANCHESTER UNITED. THE 'ASHTON REPORTER' NEWSPAPER CALLED IT 'A PLEASANT GAME' – WHICH IS ALL ANYONE CAN REALLY HOPE FOR.

• MANCHESTER CITY •

SHAUN WRIGHT-PHILLIPS

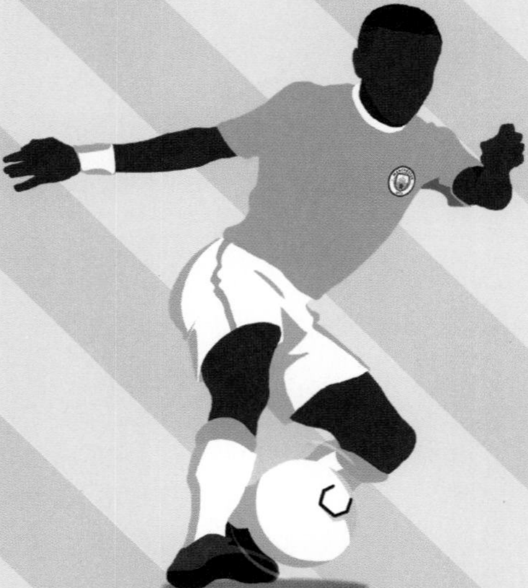

Shaun Wright-Phillips had two stints at Manchester City, but in some ways, it could have been two different clubs. He initially signed for City in 1999 from Nottingham Forest while still a youth player, joining a team that was yo-yoing between the Premier League and the First Division (which didn't become the Championship until 2004).

In this early stage of his career, City's final days at Maine Road and first days at the City of Manchester Stadium, Wright-Phillips gradually established himself as a first-team player, making 153 league appearances and finding the net 26 times. He made a further 28 appearances in other competitions, and scored an additional five goals as City consolidated their mid-table credibility.

He then had a three-season stint at Chelsea, who were enjoying their first flush of millennial success under José Mourinho, but he returned to City at the start of the 2008/09 season and helped the team start along the road from mid-table to serious title contenders. He made a further 64 league appearances in his second stint at City between 2008 and 2011, finding the net nine times.

Wright-Phillips also won 36 England caps, scoring six times, between 2004 and 2010.

WHO'S IN THE BIG
★ CHAIR TODAY? ★

There's a misconception about Manchester City. It is often thought that they burn through managers like a footballer tears through socks, that prior to the last three incumbents, no one lasts in the City technical area for very long. It's actually not strictly true for most of the Premier League era.

Discounting the four caretaker managers who have come in as stopgaps, City have enjoyed the services of 13 managers over the last 30 years, only one of which has had less than a year to stamp their authority on the team (Steve Coppell resigned of his own accord after 33 days in charge in 1996 citing the stress of the job).

That's slightly more than Liverpool's nine permanent managers, but Chelsea have had ~~19~~, ~~20~~, 21 over the same period, and Tottenham have had 17, 18, 19. Obviously, Arsenal and Manchester United are special cases, but it does suggest that even before the modern era at City, the reputation for turmoil is a little unfair. So long as you overlook the mid-1990s when, for a brief period, Maine Road ran out of paint from changing the initials on the manager's parking place.

On average, during the history of the Premier League, City has stuck by its managers for around two and a quarter years each. That's basically four or five transfer windows to get their teams in order, which seems, when it comes down to it, like a not unreasonable length of time.

There are a lot of different factors that go into creating a successful football team: players are important, luck is fundamental, but having the talent in the touchline and changing room – and that includes both the manager and the people that they surround themselves with – is what turns a group of individuals into a team. And once you've got a team, you have a chance of turning them into legends.

Season	Month hired	Manager
1990/91	Nov 1990	Peter Reid
1993/94	Aug-93	Tony Book (caretaker)
1993/94	Aug-93	Brian Horton
1995/96	Jun-95	Alan Ball
1996/97	Aug-96	Asa Hartford (caretaker)
1996/97	Oct-96	Steve Coppell
1996/97	Nov-96	Phil Neal (caretaker)
1996/97	Dec-96	Frank Clark
1998/99	Feb-98	Joe Royle
2000/01	May-01	Kevin Keegan
2004/05	Mar-05	Stuart Pearce
2007/08	Jul-07	Sven-Göran Eriksson
2008/09	Jun-08	Mark Hughes
2009/10	Dec-09	Roberto Mancini
2012/13	May-13	Brian Kidd (caretaker)
2013/14	Jun-13	Manuel Pellegrini
2016/17	Jul-16	Pep Guardiola

"I HAD TO TAKE HIM ON AT THE SAME TIME AS MY OWN BOARD. IT WAS LIKE FIGHTING MIKE TYSON WITH ONE HAND BEHIND MY BACK."

Peter Reid on managing City while Manchester United were being managed by Alex Ferguson. On the one hand, that's probably fair, but on the other, how well would Peter Reid have done against Mike Tyson even if he had both hands available?

129

VINCENT KOMPANY

Vincent Kompany joined Manchester City in 2008, having come up though the youth set up at Belgium's Anderlecht and then spending a couple of seasons with Hamburg in Germany.

On a dreary October evening in 2012, Kompany and a handful of his City teammates were heading back to Manchester from Europe, where they'd played Ajax the night before. At around 8.00 pm they got on a train at London Euston destined for Milton Keynes, gateway to the north, where they presumably thought they could connect with a fast train to Manchester. Unfortunately for them, they'd got on a local commuter train, which was going to take its own sweet time getting to Milton Keynes. The chances are that they would miss the connection to Manchester as a result.

The only other person in that carriage that evening had had a long day and didn't work out what was going on until the train had left the station, by which time it was too late to do anything. They'd like to take this opportunity to apologise.

Kompany was a phenomenal defender and an exceptional captain, making 360 appearances for City and winning 89 caps for Belgium. He is now also doing very well as manager for Burnley.

Never trust him with a train timetable though.

★ THE GAP ★

Some statistics present a challenge. Turning them into a story can be a struggle, involving slicing the data in very specific ways and then shoehorning a narrative around it so that it matches the tale that you are trying to tell.

There's none of that with Manchester City and the gap. The story tells itself. When the Premier League started, City were well off the pace; there was a gulf between the number of points the winners had and the number that City had managed to cobble together. If it was a good year, the gap was only 30 points wide, but sometimes there were whole divisions difference.

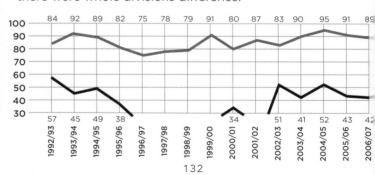

It changed at the end of the 2000s, and suddenly, for whatever reason, City weren't just competitive, they were winners. During the whole of the Premier League, the average point difference between City and the winners has been 24 points. Over the last decade, it's been seven points, and over the last five years, it's been four points.

And you can say what you like about financial firepower, but City are also taking the Premier League to new heights. In the first quarter of a century of the Premier League, the highest number of points needed to become champions was 95. The average was 86. Over the last five years, the average has been 95. Even in 2019/20 – when City didn't win it – the winners got 99 points.

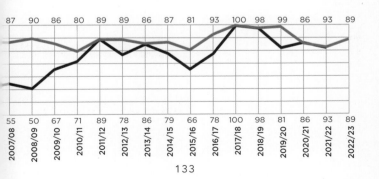

| 87 | 90 | 86 | 80 | 89 | 89 | 86 | 87 | 81 | 93 | 100 | 98 | 99 | 86 | 93 | 89 |

| 55 | 50 | 67 | 71 | 89 | 78 | 86 | 79 | 66 | 78 | 100 | 98 | 81 | 86 | 93 | 89 |

2007/08 2008/09 2009/10 2010/11 2011/12 2012/13 2013/14 2014/15 2015/16 2016/17 2017/18 2018/19 2019/20 2020/21 2021/22 2022/23

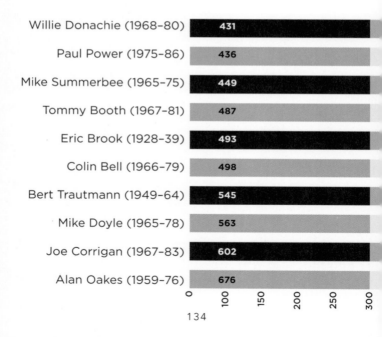

Willie Donachie (1968–80) — 431
Paul Power (1975–86) — 436
Mike Summerbee (1965–75) — 449
Tommy Booth (1967–81) — 487
Eric Brook (1928–39) — 493
Colin Bell (1966–79) — 498
Bert Trautmann (1949–64) — 545
Mike Doyle (1965–78) — 563
Joe Corrigan (1967–83) — 602
Alan Oakes (1959–76) — 676

0 · 100 · 150 · 200 · 250 · 300

MANCHESTER CITY'S TOP TEN FIRST TEAM ★ STARTS ★

(ALL COMPETITIONS)

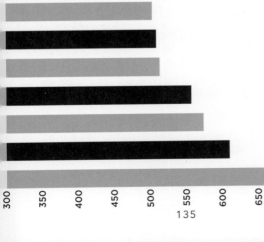

300 350 400 450 500 550 600 650 700

★ VOSSI HYPERNOVAE ★

Badly Drawn Boy, The Doves, Joy Division, Oasis, The Smiths, The Stone Roses ... the list of iconic bands of the 1980s and 1990s with members who have professed their love for Manchester City is long and distinguished.

While other teams have humiliating trips into the recording studio to record some tawdry cash-grab to celebrate nearly winning the FA Cup, City have always enjoyed the support of credible musicians, some of whom you might even want to listen to.

There's probably not much a of PhD in this: the two simple reasons are that City has a hard-won reputation as a club for the working people of Manchester, and it's a club of perennial outsiders that has always shunned the glittering lights that – until recently – always seemed to be shining brightly just outside the confines of the city's borders.

There is only one thing that has changed more than Manchester City over the last couple of decades, and that's the music scene. So, while there's a question about how the team's current levels of success will impact their support among the nation's guitar-wielding miserabilists, in the end, none of it matters. The world has changed, guitar music has become niche and everything's awesome.

NOEL GALLAGHER, THE OASIS SINGER AND SONGWRITER, IS A GOOD FRIEND OF PEP GUARDIOLA. HE CONDUCTED PEP'S FIRST INTERVIEW AS CITY'S MANAGER AND HIS SONG WONDERWALL IS PLAYED AS THE TEAM ENTER THE DRESSING ROOM ON MATCH DAY. PEP EVEN INVITED NOEL TO BRING HIS GUITAR INTO THE CHANGING ROOM AT THE END OF THE SEASON, ALTHOUGH NOEL DECLINED.

• MANCHESTER CITY •

★ YAYA TOURÉ ★

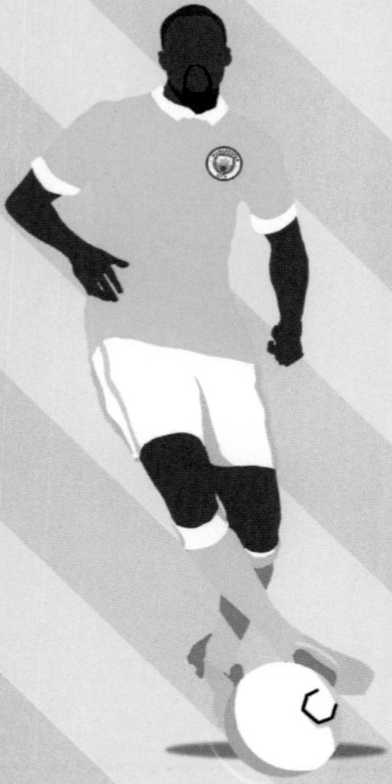

Yaya Touré graced Manchester City's team between 2010 and 2018, making 292 appearances and scoring 81 goals in all competitions. He cut his teeth at Olympiacos, Monaco and Barcelona before coming to Manchester in search of some proper weather.

His hard work and application played a pivotal midfield role as City learned how to win in the 2010s. He helped the team to victory in the Premier League three times, the League Cup twice and the FA Cup once. He was playing as the world of big data collided with football, so we know without a shadow of a doubt that in the 2013/14 season he made 1,169 successful passes in total, which averages out at 76.41 passes per game, and achieved an average passing accuracy of 90.76%. These are important statistics that the public have a right to know.

Never mind the data, Touré provided goals that were spectacular to watch, from both set pieces and open play. He also inspired an exceptionally efficient chant that rocked the terraces and was set to 2 Unlimited's high-octane Eurodance classic '*No Limit*'. It takes a while to learn the words, though.

THE PROBLEM ★ WITH PLASTICS ★

There have been two main teams in or around Manchester since the start of the 20th century, and as their fortunes have ebbed and flowed, so has their level of support. It's something that happens to every team in every town in every sport in every part of the world.

The simple truth is that the more success you have, the more fans you attract. The trouble is, though, that many of those new fans haven't suffered the pain of a 4–0 drubbing on a drizzly Tuesday night at a threadbare stadium somewhere in an industrial estate in an obscure part of the Midlands and then struggled back up the M6 at midnight to get to work in the morning. Particularly when half of your colleagues support the other team down the road and are feeling all bright-eyed and bushy-tailed and full of tales about their latest European adventure ("Oh, you should have seen the fountains!").

These new fans just don't understand the pain, the ignominy, that comes from following a team that has struggled to find success for decades. Now the shoe is on the other foot; it's the blue side of the city that's attracting the fair-weather fans, and, frankly, they get in the way. They don't know the songs and they don't know when to sing them, let alone why.

The thing is, though, at its heart, football is a form of entertainment, and if the entertainment's good, it will attract more people. More people means more money coming into the club, which means the club can afford more talent, and more talent reduces the risk of having to endure the pain of a 4–0 drubbing on a drizzly Tuesday night at a tired-out stadium somewhere in an industrial estate in an obscure part of the Midlands and then struggling back up the M6 at midnight to get to work in the morning.

If you've ever been to London and had someone tut at you for standing on the wrong side of the escalator because they are so busy and important that they need to save themselves two seconds by not waiting politely, then you know how those poor plastics feel when they hear you moaning about them on the terraces. Without them and their money, the team would find it more difficult to invest in the future, because no matter how deep the chairman's pockets, no matter how good the team is today, it changes with each passing season; clubs need to keep investing if they are going to stay at the top, and it can change very quickly. Just ask Chelsea. Or Liverpool. Or Manchester United. Or City in the 1970s.

Frankly, if you want to see the fountains, you've got to put up with the plastics.

WHEN OLD TRAFFORD WAS DAMAGED
DURING WORLD WAR II, MANCHESTER
UNITED USED THE FACILITIES AT
MAINE ROAD FOR SEVERAL YEARS.
UNITED WERE NEVER ALLOWED TO
USE THE HOME TEAM CHANGING ROOM
DURING A DERBY, THOUGH.

"SOMETIMES WE'RE GOOD AND SOMETIMES WE'RE BAD BUT WHEN WE'RE GOOD, AT LEAST WE'RE MUCH BETTER THAN WE USED TO BE AND WHEN WE ARE BAD WE'RE JUST AS BAD AS WE USED TO BE SO THAT'S GOT TO BE GOOD, HASN'T IT?"

Disk jockey Mark Radcliffe takes a philosophical view of City's resurgence.

• MANCHESTER CITY •

★ SERGIO AGÜERO ★

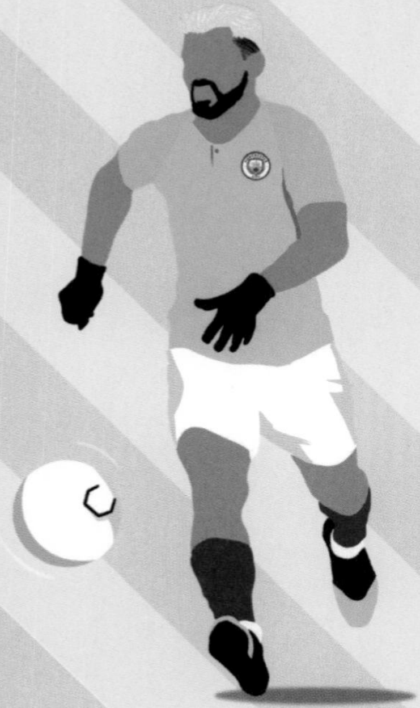

Sergio Agüero joined Manchester City in 2011 and spent a decade delighting the terraces of the Etihad, becoming the club's all-time record scorer in the process. And not just by a couple of goals either: Agüero found the net 260 times for City in all competitions; second on the list, Eric Brook (see page 18), scored 177. The only other player in the Premier League era to make it on to the top 10 is Raheem Sterling, who delivered 131 goals. Which is still impressive.

The list of achievements and accolades that Agüero received is long and impactful, and plenty of the records that he set are likely to last for a very long time. One stat that jumps out, though, is his 18 hat-tricks, 12 of which came in the Premier League, all of which broke other people's hearts.

Agüero's recent retirement, at the relatively young age of 33, was a real loss to the world of football, but it does leave him with more time to come up with a satisfying name for that third goal against Huddersfield in 2018. Back-heeled volley? Gravity defying? Rude? Phenomenal.

Then, of course, there was that goal at the end of the 2011/12 season. Legendary.

THE OPPOSITION: ⋆ CHELSEA ⋆

The rivalry between Manchester City and Chelsea is mostly professional, and there wasn't really a lot in it until the two teams started competing for titles, trophies and players. Even then it's been fairly polite.

Chelsea are a young club (relatively), not forming until 1905, by which time City had already been around in various forms for more than a quarter of a century and won their first FA Cup (in 1903/04). The two teams first locked horns in League Division One in 1907, a 2–2 draw at Stamford Bridge, which pretty much set the tone for the finely balanced future meetings between the two. They've met 174 times in all competitions up to the 2022/23 season, with City winning just under 40% of the time, Chelsea winning just over 40% of the time and the pair drawing the remaining 20% or so of the time.

Looking at the Premier League, it's pretty much as you'd expect. Prior to the takeover, City won less than 10% of the time, but now they win around half of the time. City versus Chelsea tends to be a fairly low-scoring affair, though, with an average of under 2.5 goals scored each time the teams slug it out in the top flight. That said, there have only been three 0–0 draws between the two teams in the Premier League – all three at Stamford Bridge, which is good news if you have tickets to the Etihad.

Basically, City versus Chelsea these days is a deeply functional fixture, and often a bit nervy as the two teams face each other, usually on their way to fight for silverware elsewhere.

Without wanting to start anything, it's worth pointing out

that while plenty of people have suggested City have used their resources to buy their way to the top of the table, Chelsea have also spent massively in recent seasons but have not really managed to convert that spending into success.

This suggests that City have found a way to deploy the undoubted talent they have on the books to form a team in a way that Chelsea have not managed in recent years. Yet.

AS A PLAYER, GUARDIOLA WAS PART OF JOHAN CRUYFF'S 'DREAM TEAM' AT BARCELONA, FROM 1991-1997. IN TOTAL, HE WON LA LIGA SIX TIMES, FIVE SPANISH SUPER CUPS, TWO COPA DEL REY TROPHIES, ONE EUROPEAN CUP AND TWO EUROPEAN SUPER CUPS (NOW UEFA CUP).

"WHEN YOU SCORE,
IT'S A GREAT FEELING,
BUT TO GIVE A GREAT
PASS MEANS IT'S
SOMETHING SPECIAL
FOR ME. IT'S VERY
UNDERRATED WHAT
WE DO."

Kevin De Bruyne knows that in
a team sport individual glory
comes in many forms.

• MANCHESTER CITY •

KEVIN DE BRUYNE

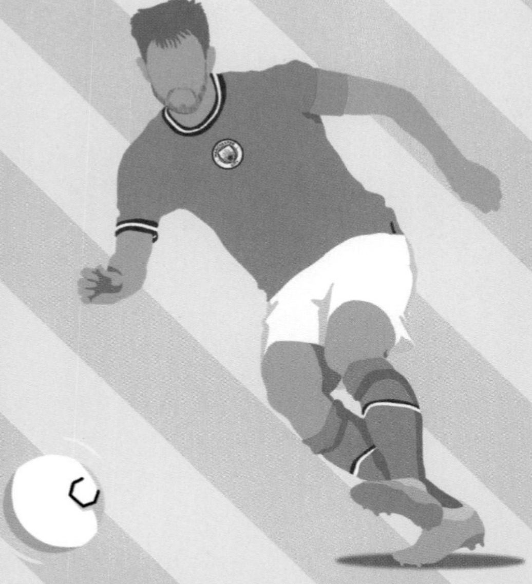

What can you say about Kevin De Bruyne? In many ways, it depends whether you are on the same team as him or are facing him.

De Bruyne started his professional career at Koninklijke Racing Club Genk, generally known to its friends as Genk, before inexplicably signing for Chelsea, where he endured three first team appearances before being loaned out to Werder Bremen. He then spent a season at VfL Wolfsberg, before joining Manchester City at the start of the 2015/16 season.

He's one of those players who appears to be able to hold his own in pretty much any position, up to and including the role of team chef if his social media presence is anything to go by. Mostly, though, he appears to enjoy a role in either central midfield or slightly further forward, terrifying defenders while letting pundits really test out their collections of superlatives.

He has been capped 99 times for Belgium, scoring 26 goals so far. He became the national side's captain in 2023.

Player	Club
Bryan Robson	West Bromwich Albion, Manchester United, Middlesborough
Billy Wright	Wolverhampton Wanderers
Frank Lampard	West Ham, Chelsea, Manchester City
Bobby Charlton	Manchester United
Ashley Cole	Arsenal, Chelsea, Derby County
Bobby Moore	West Ham, Fulham
Steven Gerrard	Liverpool
David Beckham	Manchester United
Wayne Rooney	Everton, Manchester United, Deby County
Peter Shilton	Leicester City, Stoke City, Nottingham Forest, Southampton, Derby County, Plymouth Argyle, Wimbledon, Bolton Wanderers, Coventry City, West Ham United, Leyton Orient

Caps

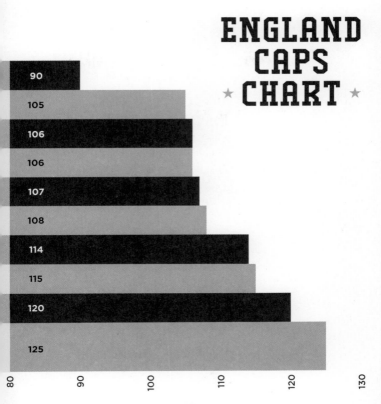

ENGLAND CAPS ★ CHART ★

90
105
106
106
107
108
114
115
120
125

80 90 100 110 120 130

• MANCHESTER CITY •

PEP GUARDIOLA

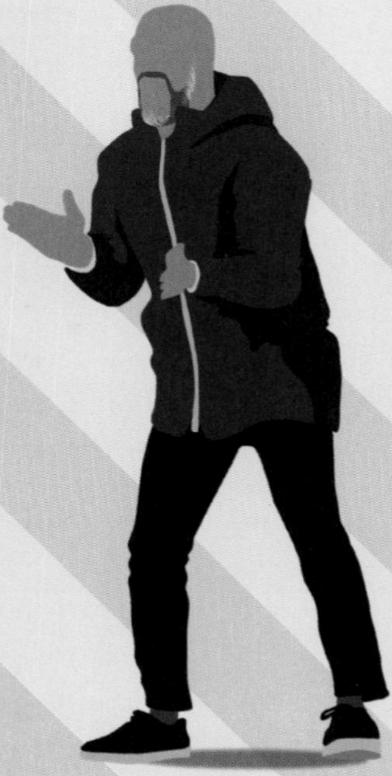

Every manager is different: there are the dour ones, the ones who have seen it all before, there are the ones who stalk the touchline and the ones who look like rabbits caught in headlights. But Pep Guardiola is one of those rarest of things: a manager who seems to be genuinely enjoying himself.

To be fair, if someone gave pretty much any of us the keys to the Etihad and asked us to manage the club, we'd probably have a great time for a month or two. But then the weight of expectation would start to get to us and we'd stop smiling. Guardiola, though, has been in post for more than seven years, and most days he still appears to be having a good time.

He also seems to know how to get the best out of his players. All right, if we were going to be hypercritical, it could be suggested that some of what he comes out with flirts with the kind of management-speak that wouldn't seem out of place in a London consultancy, and it's possible that maybe he says 'guys' too often, but his record speaks for itself.

He arrived at City having won both La Liga in Spain and the Bundesliga in Germany three times apiece, and has now won the Premier League five times. He's won cups aplenty, and that's before we even go into his playing career, which is frankly too glittering to fit into the space that we have here.

There was really only one thing that eluded him in terms of honours earned while managing an English club, and on June 10, 2023 he brought the Champions League trophy home to Manchester, dismantling Real Madrid 5-1 on aggregate in the semi-final.

What Guardiola has shown is that it is possible to achieve greatness without resorting to being either miserable, defensive or overly aggressive. Perhaps a few members of the British government should take notes.

There are those that say that Guardiola has now won every possible accolade in English football, but there are always more records to be broken. 14 Premier League titles and three Champions Leagues – that would be an achievement.

"CREATING SOMETHING NEW IS THE DIFFICULT PART. TO MAKE IT AND BUILD IT AND GET EVERYONE TO FOLLOW? AMAZING."

Guardiola has earned a moment of pride.

WHAT'S THE POINT
★ OF THE D? ★

The D attached to the penalty area often just seems to be there, not really doing much other than making the box a bit more aesthetically pleasing – but it does actually serve a practical purpose.

Officially known as the very grand sounding 'penalty arc', it marks the edge of a 9.14-metre (10-yard) circle around the penalty spot which players can't go into when a penalty is being taken. It's the only part of this circle that is outside the penalty area, which is why it's the only part that is painted on to the turf. It basically means that no player can take an unfair advantage by being able to stand closer to the penalty spot than anyone other than the penalty taker, which can be important if players are competing for the ball if there's a rebound.

The goalkeeper cannot handle the ball in the penalty arc, opposition players can stand in it when a goal kick is being taken and if a foul is committed in the D then the best/ worst that the ref will give is a free kick, but having it there means that there's one less thing to argue about when a penalty is awarded.

The Video Assistant Referee (VAR) system has of course refined the rules/complicated matters. In 2021, Ederson skilfully blocked a spot kick from Everton's Gylfi Sigurdsson and the ball was put clear by Kyle Walker, but anyone watching the match could see that several players had encroached on the D before the penalty was taken.

The reason the penalty was not retaken was that VAR judged none of the encroaching players had actually interfered with play in the aftermath of the penalty. Have we enhanced your understanding?

GLAUBER BERTI BECAME A CITY LEGEND AFTER A CAREER PLAYING JUST SIX MINUTES IN ONE GAME DURING THE 2008/09 SEASON BUT BEING VOTED MAN OF THE MATCH BY THE CITY FANS.

★ THE TROPHY CABINET ★

MEN

Competition	Year
First Division	1936/37, 1967/68
Premier League	2011/12, 2013/14, 2017/18, 2018/19, 2020/21, 2021/22, 2022/23
Second Division	1898/99, 1902/03, 1909/10, 1927/28, 1946/47, 1965/66
Championship	2001/02
FA Cup	1903/04, 1933/34, 1955/56, 1968/69, 2010/11, 2018/19, 2022/23
Football League Cup EFL Cup	1969/70, 1975/76, 2013/14, 2015/16, 2017/18, 2018/19, 2019/20, 2020/21
FA Charity Shield Community Shield	1937, 1968, 1972, 2012, 2018, 2019
UEFA Cup Winners' Cup	1969/70,
UEFA Champions League	2022/23

WOMEN

Competition	Year
FA Women's Super League Champions	2016
Women's FA Cup Winners	2016-17, 2018/19, 2019/20